Fistfuls of Dollars:

Fact and Fantasy About Corporate Charitable Giving

First Edition

EarthWrites Publishing

Redondo Beach, California 90277

Linda M. Zukowski

Fistfuls of Dollars: Fact and Fantasy About Corporate Charitable Giving
by Linda M. Zukowski

Published by: EarthWrites, 409 N. Pacific Coast Hwy. #423, Redondo Beach, California 90277

Grateful acknowledgement is made to the following for permission to reprint previously published material:

• Giving USA

• The Foundation Center

Library of Congress Cataloging-In-Publication Data
Zukowski, Linda M.
    Fistfuls of Dollars: Fact and Fantasy About Corporate Charitable Giving /
    Linda M. Zukowski

Includes bibliographical references and index.

ISBN: 0-9661314-2-8
1. Fund raising   2. Non-profit Organizations—Finance   I. Title
Library of Congress Catalog Card Number: 97-94993

 This book is printed on recycled, acid-free paper.

To Becky Loving,
for guiding me along the path

Table of Contents

Forward

It's been said that most people go through two or three different careers in their lifetime. As my friends never stop reminding me, I'm well on my way to beating that number. You see, I started out planning to become a teacher. I taught and supervised the special education program in a junior and senior high school on the East Coast for a few years.

Later, I found myself moving across the country to California where I worked as a manager in a large corporation for almost 12 years. The promotions and the increases in salary came at appropriate intervals, and for awhile that was enough. But a nagging need to have more of a purpose, to create something that really mattered, eventually pushed me out the corporate door and into the world of non-profits.

A stint as a non-profit volunteer, stuffing envelopes, answering phones, organizing events, and even fund raising gave me a healthy respect for the enormity of the task confronting most non-profit organizations. I soon realized that the planning, organizing, financial and human resources skills I had gained from working in a corporation were critically needed in the non-profit sector. So now as a consultant, I have found the creative purpose that had eluded me for so many years. I have learned to use my corporate skills and experiences to improve the effectiveness of non-profit agencies and help these organizations create positive and lasting changes in society.

This book is a marriage of my experience in corporations with my current work in the non-profit arena. It summarizes six months of interviews with corporate managers about their companies' charitable giving programs and is designed to help non-profit agencies improve their chances of obtaining corporate support. The information contained in these pages is not my opinion, although I do occasionally supplement the material with a comment or two. It is primarily a summary of the thoughts, ideas, and suggestions of the people actually involved in deciding where corporations will spend their charitable dollars. Their comments provide invaluable information for anyone trying to attract corporate funding for a non-profit program.

Just a small grammatical comment. In recognition of the fact that both men and women are actively involved in corporate and non-profit management, I have chosen to use masculine and feminine pronouns interchangeably throughout this book when referring to corporate managers and non-profit staff members.

I hope this book answers most of your questions about corporate charitable giving. Good luck with your fund raising!

Acknowledgements

I want to thank Carol Sugimura for providing me with the first research contacts and for her initial editing work. Carol, you got me started. I also want to thank Carol for her ongoing inspiration. She was always certain this project would be completed—even when I was doubtful.

I want to thank Deidre Hicks for her encouragement and willingness to listen to my ideas, at any time of the day or night. Deidre's unflagging enthusiasm was a constant source of motivation.

I want to thank Constance Beutel for her work with the initial editing and graphics. I also want to acknowledge her imagination and vision. Whenever my thinking became narrow and limited, Constance nudged me forward by reminding me of the possibilities.

I want to thank each of the corporate representatives who participated in the research for this book. (The names of the participating corporations are listed in the appendix.) Their decision to discuss corporate giving practices at their companies was a purely voluntary one. As a former corporate manager, I am very familiar with the demands on their time and I am, therefore, even more grateful for their involvement.

Finally, I want to thank Lee Jackman for introducing me to the world of non-profits and the joys of fund raising.

"We make a living by what we get,
but we make a life by what we give."

—Winston Churchill

CHAPTER I
Introduction

☞ Overview

Congratulations on picking up this book! If the title interested you, you're probably involved to some degree with non-profit organizations and you're probably also trying to make some positive changes to society. It sounds like a big job and it is. Your actions are helping to create solutions to difficult problems, although there may be some days when you wonder if you're having any impact at all.

Bringing something good into this society, no matter how positive the results or how many people are helped, is not without a price tag. If you are like most people involved with the non-profit sector, you are probably searching for a way to finance your good works.

While you're out there looking for financial assistance for your non-profit program, there are many corporations looking for charitable issues to support. In increasing numbers, companies are recognizing the value of charitable contributions to the ongoing success of their business. However, companies do not fund every request they receive from a non-profit organization.

> **In order to receive corporate funding, you must understand how to ask a corporation for support.**

Anyone who has sought funding from corporations knows that the charitable interests of companies are as varied as the companies themselves. Charitable giving programs are frequently modified whenever the companies experience change of any kind. Mergers, fluctuations in stock prices, introductions of new products, changes in executive management, unexpected losses or gains all may have an impact on the size, type and the very existence of a particular company's charitable giving program. Therefore, this book will not identify the specific projects funded by any company. That type of specific information is best obtained by contacting the company directly and requesting their charitable giving guidelines.

Instead, this book will help non-profits, both seasoned agencies and new grassroots groups, better understand the general process of corporate charitable giving and identify the most effective methods of tapping into this funding stream. This book will provide tips on beginning or improving your efforts to obtain corporate funding. It will explain the overall process of corporate charitable giving and define the most effective methods of writing corporate grant proposals. The book will identify the misconceptions, the **fantasies,** about corporate funding and provide the **facts** you need to successfully attract corporate interest in your programs.

☞ The Corporate Paradox

Although most people would agree that corporations have had a profound impact on society, it would be difficult to obtain consensus on the value of that impact. Corporations are sometimes considered the root of all societal evils while concurrently held up as the last, best hope for a better world. Many of us depend on corporations for our livelihood and yet we frequently hold corporations responsible for many of society's problems. The involvement and the lack of involvement by corporations in charitable giving is also subject to debate.

Do corporations have a responsibility to society or are they responsible only to their employees, customers or stockholders? Can and should corporations be expected to increase their charitable funding according to the size of their profits? Is corporate support of charitable programs done out of concern for public welfare or is it just a public relations tool? Does corporate charitable giving unfairly determine the type of non-profit agencies available in a community? Does the motivation and the size of charitable donations really matter; isn't the mere existence of corporate charitable giving commendable in itself?

Although any of these questions could be the subject of its own book, you won't find any of them addressed in the following pages. This book is not designed to judge the motivations of any company or evaluate the effectiveness of corporate charitable giving programs. Its purpose is not to decide if a company's charitable giving program is helpful, complicated or even equitable.

This book is designed to provide you with practical suggestions for obtaining corporate support of your non-profit programs.

The following chapters will separate the facts from the fantasies by correcting common misunderstandings about corporate philan-thropy and providing insight into how decisions to fund non-profits are made. It provides a "behind the scenes tour" of corporate chari-table giving and offers practical recommendations to improve the next proposal you are planning to send to a company.

Using input from the corporate employees responsible for the charitable giving programs in their companies, this book offers suggestions to help non-profit agencies successfully contact corpora-tions, develop effective relationships and create winning proposals. What you learn from the following pages may not solve all of your money problems, but it will increase your chances of obtaining corporate funding for your non-profit projects.

☞ Content

Requesting corporate support is a competitive process. It requires knowing how to effectively approach a corporation and how to present a case that offers something of value to that corporation. The following chapters will take you through the corporate char-itable giving process from the perspective of those who manage the charitable funding processes in their companies. The following aspects of corporate giving will be addressed in detail:

• the reasons for corporate philanthropy and the implications for your proposal

- the processes used by most corporations to select non-profit agencies for funding

- the most effective methods of approaching and interacting with corporations

- corporate perspectives on funding of newly established non-profit agencies

- the attributes of successful corporate proposals

- program objectives and evaluation

- budgets and financial information

- the importance of a non-profit's leadership

- the role of site-visits

- responding to a company's funding decision

> **If you have already begun writing a proposal to a corporation and are looking for some quick advice, the last chapter contains a summary of suggestions from corporate funders. You may want to review this chapter before submitting your proposal.**

☞ Sources of Information

The material in this book is based on interviews with corporate representatives who are involved with the actual decisions to fund non-profit agencies. In targeting companies for this research, I interviewed representatives from 37 different corporations over a period of six months. (See Appendix 1 for a list of participating corporations.) I targeted companies with well-established, rather than newly formed, corporate foundations or corporate giving programs in order to benefit from their years of experience with grantmaking. I focused on companies that are headquartered or have a significant impact in California and the Pacific Northwest, since this is the region where I have the most familiarity, having worked, lived and traveled there extensively.

However, most of the companies that participated in this research are National or International in scope and they fund non-profit programs throughout the country. Therefore, the general content of this book is applicable to most non-profit organizations, regardless of location. Finally, I chose companies from a variety of different industries to ensure the data obtained was representative of the general process of corporate charitable giving.

Of the 37 participating corporations, a total of 28 were interviewed in face-to-face meetings at their corporate headquarters; the other corporate representatives were interviewed by phone. Three of the companies were interviewed twice, with different managers, each with distinct responsibilities in terms of geography and scope.

In addition to these detailed interviews, all the companies were asked to complete a short questionnaire providing quantifiable support of the issues discussed. Thirty-eight managers, representing 35 companies, responded to that questionnaire. Responses to the questionnaire have been plotted on graphs and appear throughout the book to supplement the various concepts. The entire questionnaire and regional results can be found in Appendix 2.

Managers interviewed for this book represent both corporate foundations and corporate giving programs. However, no significant differences in administration of these programs were noted, and so their input has been consolidated into the materials presented here.

None of the participating companies placed any restrictions on the interviews or the manner in which the material was ultimately presented. The companies that participated in the research for this book were not compensated, nor did they review the content prior to publishing. Prior to the interviews, and in an attempt to ensure candor from all participants, I informed the corporate representatives that their individual comments would remain anonymous. Therefore, the quotations that appear in the following chapters are actual comments from the corporate representatives, but they are not identified by source.

Since the information in this book is a summary of a series of interviews and questionnaires, any reader who requires specific information about a particular company's charitable funding program should contact that company directly.

☞ The Limits of Corporate Funding

Before you consider abandoning all other types of fund raising and begin to focus solely on corporate giving, you should realize that corporate support alone will not fund all your expenses. The most common fantasy about corporate funding involves the amount of money and the size of grants contributed by companies to charities. Most corporations contribute less to charitable issues than you might think. In fact, only about 5.6% of all charitable giving in 1996 came from corporations. Individuals, not corporations, were the source of most charitable giving. (See Figure 1.1.) Although there are instances where corporations have donated hundreds of thousands, or even millions of dollars to charities, the average corporate grant tends to be small. Unless yours is a nationally known and well-respected program, or unless you have very strong personal connections with a company, you can expect the average, one-year corporate grant to be less than $10,000.

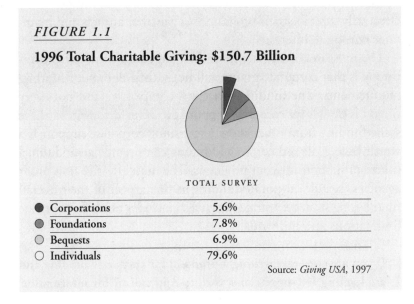

FIGURE 1.1

1996 Total Charitable Giving: $150.7 Billion

TOTAL SURVEY

● Corporations	5.6%
● Foundations	7.8%
○ Bequests	6.9%
○ Individuals	79.6%

Source: *Giving USA*, 1997

The comparatively small amount of corporate charitable giving is partly due to the fact that corporations have enormous liabilities. In addition to the basic cost of doing business, labor costs, buildings, equipment, etc., there is an expectation that the company's stock will increase in value and stockholders will periodically receive dividends. Corporate executives must use the company's revenue to keep the company growing and the shareholders satisfied, or they risk losing their jobs.

However, these numbers shouldn't dissuade you from investigating and pursuing corporate funding. While it is true that the **percentage** of corporate charitable giving is smaller than other sources of charitable giving, the **total amount** of money given to charitable causes by corporations is significant.

> **The 5.6% of total charitable giving attributed to corporations in 1996 is equal to about $8.5 billion!**[1]

These dollars are available to non-profit organizations that can effectively describe their program in a way that attracts and maintains corporate interest.

The most important fact to understand about corporate philanthropy is that corporate grants will not satisfy all of your funding requirements. The funding process is competitive and not every project is eligible for corporate support. However, if you already have some funding from other sources, pursuing corporate support is a worthwhile goal; and corporate funding can become an additional source of support for your programs. The most effective non-profit agencies include corporate funding as one aspect of their overall fund raising strategy; a strategy that also includes funds from private foundations and individuals.

> **If you are currently writing a proposal for corporate funding and are looking for suggestions, turn to Appendix 7 for information on how you can receive a FREE critique of your proposal.**

[1] *Susan Gray, "Americans' Gifts Top $150 Billion,"* The Chronicle of Philanthropy. *June 12, 1997, p. 39.*

Chapter 2

The Reasons for
Corporate Philanthropy

☞ Definitions of Charitable Giving Structures

Corporations generally administer their charitable giving through a corporate foundation, a corporate giving program or a combination of both. Each may have a different application process, and the size and type of grants they distribute may differ. Many times the corporate foundation and the corporate giving program share the same staff, although some companies keep these functions administratively separate. To avoid confusing a company's charitable giving programs, the reader should be certain to thoroughly research and follow the company's procedures when submitting any request for funding.

The following are definitions of corporate giving structures and other common types of foundations:

1. Company-Sponsored Foundation (also referred to as Corporate Foundation)

A private foundation whose grant funds are derived primarily from the contributions of a profit-making business organization. The corporate foundation may maintain close ties with the donor company, but it is an independent organization with its own endowment and is subject to the same rules and regulations as other private foundations.[2]

---

[2] National Guide to Funding for the Environment & Animal Welfare *(New York, N.Y.: The Foundation Center, 1994), p. xvii.*

Trustees of the corporate foundation frequently include senior executives of the corporation. Corporate foundation giving is generally administered through grantmaking and, like other foundations, corporate foundations publish annual reports and guidelines detailing the procedures for submitting proposals.

2. Corporate Giving Program or Direct Corporate Giving

A grantmaking program established and administered within a profit-making company. Corporate giving programs do not have a separate endowment and their annual grant totals are generally more related to current company profits. They are not subject to the same reporting requirements as private foundations.[3]

In addition to cash contributions, direct corporate giving includes "in-kind" donations, which are non-cash gifts of goods and service. Donations of company products, supplies and equipment are the most common forms of in-kind giving, although in-kind support can also include technical assistance and use of office space.

Corporate giving programs may also be administered through grantmaking, although if the company also has a foundation, the corporate giving grants are usually smaller than those distributed by the foundation. Corporate giving programs tend to be more interested, than corporate foundations, in sponsorship of local special events.

Many corporations have both a corporate foundation and a corporate giving program. Be careful not to confuse the two when you are communicating with the corporate representatives. Unless otherwise indicated, the information in this book pertains to both corporate foundations and corporate giving programs.

---

[3] *The Foundation Center, p. xvii.*

3. Private Foundations

A non governmental, non-profit organization with funds (usually from a single source, such as an individual, family or corporation) and programs managed by its own trustees or directors that was established to maintain or aid social, educational, religious or other charitable activities serving the common welfare, primarily through the making of grants.

4. Family Foundation

An independent private foundation whose funds are derived from members of a single family. Family members often serve as officers or board members of the foundation and have a significant role in grantmaking decisions.

5. Community Foundation

A 501(c)(3) organization that makes grants for charitable purposes in a specific community or region. Funds are usually derived from many donors and held in an endowment independently administered; income earned by the endowment is then used to make grants. Although a few community foundations may be classified by the IRS as private foundations, most are classified as public charities eligible for maximum income tax deductible contributions from the general public.[4]

☞ Matching Gift Programs

Although not as well-known and often under-utilized, matching gift programs can be an effective source of corporate funding. Programs of this type are becoming more prevalent among large corporations as a way to motivate employees. By supporting their community work, the company hopes to increase the employees'

---

[4] *The Foundation Center, p. xvii-xix.*

loyalty to the company. Matching gift programs differ slightly among companies, but all essentially match the monetary charitable contribution an employee makes to a non-profit agency.

Some matching gift programs put a limit on the size of the gift to be matched, others will only match gifts made to certain types of non-profits. The size of the matching gift also differs among companies. Most match dollar for dollar, others match only half of the employee's gift, while some contribute two or three dollars for every employee dollar. Some programs match corporate dollars with each hour of time an employee volunteers with a non-profit agency. Most companies only match gifts made by active full-time employees, although there are programs that match gifts from part-time and retired employees, and sometimes even from spouses of employees.

Non-profits seeking corporate support should not ignore the potential of matching gift programs. This is a fairly "painless" way to acquire funding; there are no proposals to write and no application forms to complete. The most complicated aspect of developing a matching gift program is identifying companies having programs that match the contributions made by your individual donors. This can be time consuming, but do not let that turn you away from this potential source of funding. The time spent determining the employers of your donors and then identifying which of those companies has a matching gift program is worth the effort.

In Appendix 4 you will find resources to help you identify corporate matching gift programs. Use these resources to find companies with matching gift programs and then determine if anyone related to your agency—your volunteers, members, clients or individual donors—is an employee of those companies. If you find donors who work for a company with a matching gift program, be sure to inform them. Your donors may not realize that their employers will match their charitable gift to your agency.

Even if you have already investigated the possibility of matching gifts from your donors, remember to periodically recheck both donors and employers. Companies frequently change their matching gift policies and your donors may change jobs.

☞ Misconceptions About Corporate Charitable Giving

Whether you are a non-profit agency that has gained corporate support in the past and are now looking to increase that level of support, or you are a non-profit agency completely unfamiliar with corporations and just beginning to think about adding corporate support to your existing funding stream, an important first step is understanding the reasons corporations support non-profit agencies. A good place to start is by addressing some of the fantasies—the misconceptions—about attracting corporate funding that were mentioned by the managers I interviewed. The following were the most frequently cited misconceptions:

1. Create entirely new programs to match available corporate funding.

The first misconception about corporate charitable funding is a belief that non-profits can increase their chances of obtaining corporate support by identifying the areas funded by a particular company, and then modifying their existing programs or creating new programs more in alignment with these corporate funding areas. This may seem to be a tempting strategy, but it is usually unsuccessful. The companies I interviewed felt they were able to recognize when non-profits were "chasing corporate dollars" by adding new programs unrelated to their core focus, or stretching their mission statement just enough to fit the company's guidelines. Since it was expected that these new programs would not survive after the corporate grant had been spent, providing funding was considered to be a bad investment of corporate dollars.

Trying to stretch your program's goals or create completely new programs in an attempt to match corporate funding areas is a waste of time. Instead, search for companies whose funding interests are more in alignment with your actual programs.

2. Expect that all important charitable programs will be funded.

Another misconception is that corporations will provide a non-profit agency with financial support simply because the non-profit does such good work in the community. Instead, most companies stated that the importance of a non-profit's programs is no longer sufficient reason to provide funding. The number of non-profit organizations has increased so dramatically in recent years that it is impossible for one company to fund every important societal need. The following two quotes were typical of the comments made by corporate representatives on this issue:

> **"Gone are the days when corporate money is just given to a group doing good work. Our money is limited and there are thousands of non-profits and people in the country doing good work. We need to find a way to distinguish among them."**

> **"The size of our corporation doesn't mean we are able to fund all non-profits and all issues. There are too many non-profits out there, we have to decide how to distribute our money."**

As a non-profit seeking corporate funding, you should realize that you are competing with hundreds, and perhaps thousands, of equally qualified agencies hoping to attract the same corporate grant money. The non-profit agencies that will receive corporate funding are those best able to clearly and concisely present their program, its impact and its linkage to the interests of the company. Other factors can increase, to some extent, the possibility of funding and they will be discussed in subsequent chapters. However, without a well-conceived, professional presentation, your chances of receiving corporate support are almost non-existent.

3. Use emotional pleas.

Another well-meaning, but ineffective tactic employed by non-profit agencies is the use of emotional pleas to attract corporate sympathy. Over the years the television evening news has brought war, famine and other tragedies into our living rooms every night and, as a result, many of us have become somewhat immune to sad stories that attempt to tug at our heartstrings. The same is true for corporate funders. Corporations are rarely motivated to act by the desperate letter that begs for "any kind of help before we are forced to close our doors forever on our needy clients." A substantive program with demonstrated impact is valued by companies much more than emotional pleas.

Since emotion plays such an important role in most funding requests made by non-profits, I was interested in determining if any of the corporations made charitable grants for purely altruistic reasons and, during the interviews, I found a few companies that did. Generally, these companies were founded or managed by executives who are motivated by a belief that charitable giving is just the right thing to do. However, most companies in my research expected something more in return for their financial support. As one manager said,

> **"Corporate giving is done for reasons of enlightened self-interest. There is a desire to help the community tempered with a responsibility to shareholders. Corporate charitable giving needs to demonstrate a return to investors in lieu of dividends."**

In fact, more than half of the managers who responded to the research questionnaire indicated that charitable giving in their company was not motivated by altruism, but instead, was considered an opportunity to invest in the community. (See Figure 2.1.)

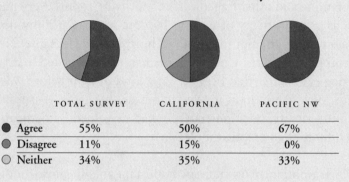

FIGURE 2.1—RESEARCH QUESTIONNAIRE

"We consider our funding of non-profit organizations to be more of a strategic business investment in the community, rather than an altruistic donation to a charity."

		TOTAL SURVEY	CALIFORNIA	PACIFIC NW
● Agree		55%	50%	67%
◐ Disagree		11%	15%	0%
○ Neither		34%	35%	33%

This has important implications for non-profits seeking corporate funding. Instead of viewing themselves as charities begging for support, non-profit agencies need to alter their own perception and begin to look at themselves as businesses. Non-profit agencies have employees, budgets and clients, and provide a needed service or product, similar to for-profit businesses. While non-profits may not generate revenue that is distributed to shareholders, they must generate sufficient income to, at least, cover their expenses.

In all interactions with corporations, it is important to think of your agency as a business, whether you make a profit or not. Remember you are dealing with people who relate to the business model and the organizational functions for marketing, operations, communications and manufacturing. Speak to these concepts when discussing your agency with a corporation.

I am not implying that attracting corporate support requires you to give up your 501(c)(3) status, issue stock certificates and require your staff to wear pinstripes. However, non-profit agencies that have successfully attracted corporate support have learned to present their agencies in a professional, business-like manner. They have learned to translate their work into concepts familiar to business people. They do not approach a corporation with a feeling of inadequacy or a belief that they are somehow "less than" the corporation. They communicate their success and their plans for continued success. They clearly, concisely and accurately communicate their needs to the company and recognize the value they offer the company in return for a charitable contribution. The successful non-profit understands the corporation's reasons for offering charitable support and can articulate how they meet those corporate needs. As one manager said,

> **"Charitable giving is similar to a business transaction; both sides need to be aware of the expectations."**

☞ The Reasons for Corporate Giving

Why do corporations give millions of dollars worth of money, time and equipment to non-profits each year? My interviews indicated that corporate giving is not a random distribution of funds, nor based solely on the whims of some high level executives. Corporate philanthropy is part of a well-conceived strategy linked to the company's overall business goals. My interviews indicated that corporations' interests in philanthropy can be categorized into five distinct areas, which I refer to as **Strategic Interests.** As a non-profit agency, your ability to attract corporate support can be enhanced by taking the time to thoroughly research a corporation to identify the strategic interests motivating their philanthropic giving.

Strategic Interests Motivating Corporate Philanthropy

1. Good Corporate Citizen

2. Influence and Relationships

3. Employee Support

4. Recognition and Brand Exposure

5. Strategic Partnerships

1. Good Corporate Citizen

Most companies indicated that their charitable giving was motivated, to some degree, by an interest in being perceived as a good
corporate citizen—a company known for supporting efforts to
improve the community. A company acting out of a desire to be
a good corporate citizen, first defines what it believes are the most
pressing needs of the community and then, targets its funding to
support those non-profit agencies that are addressing those issues.
The charitable work of a good corporate citizen projects an image
to the community of a concerned company addressing a pressing
social need. Despite the potential public relations benefits, charitable giving as a good corporate citizen is primarily done to improve
the community. It is a purely philanthropic motive and any public
relations benefits are generally of secondary importance.

Good corporate citizenship is not normally the only interest,
or even the most important interest, for any but a few of the corporations I researched. All the managers I interviewed said their
company wanted to improve the community, particularly the
communities in which they operated, and some companies even
had this goal as part of their corporate mission. Only a few companies, however, cited improvement of the community and being
known as a good corporate citizen as the **only reason** for their
company's charitable funding.

Yet, the value corporations place on being perceived as good corporate citizens should not be underestimated since it does influence,
to some extent, many corporate funding decisions. As a non-profit,
you can increase your chances of matching a strategic interest in
good corporate citizenship by ensuring that all funding requests to
corporations define the community need you are attempting to
resolve and not just the program you are offering. (This is good
rule for any proposal.)

A company, acting from a desire to be perceived as a good corporate citizen, is looking to address a pressing social need or critical
issue, and so you must clearly define the need addressed by your
program. Explaining the service provided by your agency, without

also defining the need you hope to address, will rarely attract the attention of the company interested in being recognized as a good corporate citizen.

2. Influence and Relationships

Some companies use their charitable giving to influence an individual or group of individuals who are important to the company. The company may fund a certain issue, such as the environment, AIDS, elementary education or a particular non-profit agency, because of the expected good will that might result from their contribution. These companies want their charitable funding to influence important community members, decision makers, customers, political leaders or anyone with a stake in their business or the way their business is operated.

> **Companies with a strategic interest in generating influence also want to make a positive impact in the community. But unlike the good corporate citizen, these companies expect something in return for their contributions.**

Utilities, banks, airlines and other industries impacted by regulation may look to their charitable giving programs to assist their attempts to lobby the legislature. They may, for example, look to fund a non-profit agency that is a particular favorite of a politician developing legislation affecting the company. Non-regulated industries are more likely to use charitable funding to influence a specific customer set or a particular geographic area that has been targeted as a new market. Charitable giving to selected agencies can also be effective when confronted with a short-term threat, such as trying to defuse negative media attention related to a company's manufacturing processes or their treatment of their employees, or reports of quality or safety problems with their product.

Although all companies in my interviews acknowledged that they hoped their charitable funding generated influence and good will among the public, most indicated this was much less important to corporations than non-profits generally believed. It seems that charitable giving in exchange for influence is most important only for certain industries and only at certain times, and is not an ongoing factor in most corporations' charitable funding decisions. The entire issue of charitable funding and relationships will be discussed in Chapter 4, but it is mentioned here because the ability to generate influence, although not a primary factor, still is a strategic interest guiding the charitable funding decisions of a few companies.

If, as a non-profit, you have influential community members on your board or you are connected with decision makers, you should certainly note this in your proposal to a company. However, do not expect influential connections to make up for an ill-conceived project or a poorly articulated proposal. In order to be funded, your project must still meet the company's guidelines and you must still be able to describe how it effectively impacts a community need.

3. Employee Support

The ability of a company to recruit and retain high-quality employees is an important competitive advantage, especially for high-tech firms and companies with jobs that require specialized skill sets. Training employees is expensive and the cost is compounded when the trained employees decide to take their skills to a competing firm. Companies that can attract skilled employees and, once hired, keep those employees motivated and excited about their jobs, can direct more of their resources to improving their position in the marketplace, and less on having to continually compensate for high employee turnover.

The impact of employee satisfaction on bottom-line performance has long been recognized by corporations as they spend millions of dollars each year on the latest technique for increasing morale and loyalty to the company. Quality circles, team building, self-managed teams and consensus management are all attempts to involve employees in decision making and increase corporate loyalty.

Some companies believe charitable giving programs can also have a positive impact on their efforts to improve employee relations.

Like most of us, employees of large corporations want to live in a community with a strong infrastructure—with services such as high-quality schools, medical care, mass transportation, recreation and arts programs. Some companies support non-profit agencies that provide these types of services, most likely to be used by employees and their families. There is an expectation that the company's charitable giving program will strengthen and improve these services, and thereby encourage employees to remain in the community and stay with the company.

The non-profit agencies most likely to receive this support not only provide the services used by employees, but they also tend to be located in the geographic areas where the employees live and work. Companies also expressed an interest in funding non-profit agencies that would provide vital services for employees who might fall victim to future staff reductions. Health care and child care programs were frequently cited as examples.

Corporate charitable giving was seen as supporting more than the physical needs of employees. It was felt that most employees have an innate desire to work for a company that is ethical and is concerned about more than just making profits. Employees want to be proud of their company and want to believe it is a good place to work. Corporate philanthropy fills this need by stressing the social conscience of the company and demonstrating a corporate interest in social issues of importance to employees, potentially increasing loyalty to the company.

Supporting employees who work as volunteers in non-profit agencies was also seen by companies as a way to boost their employees' morale. Many companies have specialized programs that match employees to volunteer opportunities, and most companies look more favorably on requests for financial support from agencies that have their employees working as volunteers. Employee volunteers are considered by many companies to be ambassadors for the company, providing concrete examples of the social conscience of the company which might translate into increased goodwill among consumers.

An important initial step in obtaining corporate support is attracting the interest of a company's employees in your agency and your services.

Before requesting funds from a company, contact the company's employees. Find creative ways to educate the employees about your programs and interest them in volunteer opportunities. Approach managers of local companies and request permission to leave brochures describing your work in the employees' lunchroom, or spend a few hours in the lunchroom yourself, explaining your program to employees and describing the need for volunteers. If you are planning a special event, look to local companies to provide volunteers. Consider inviting local employees to become members of your Board of Directors. If the company is unionized, contact the union representatives and request volunteer support.

Most corporate employees have little free time after their job and family responsibilities, and so they are frequently unaware of critical issues in the community, unless personally affected by them. Non-profits that take the time to explain their program and the need in the community for their program are frequently successful in securing company employees as volunteers.

Having employees as volunteers or as clients of your program will certainly increase your chances of being funded, but it is by no means a guarantee of funding. Your program still must be strong and well-presented.

Many large corporations have tens of thousands of employees and cannot possibly fund all their charitable interests. Your program must still compete with the funding requests of many other non-profits agencies and, in the end, the funding decision ultimately rests on the company's perception of the need for your program and the effectiveness of your agency.

4. Recognition and Brand Exposure

In return for charitable contributions, corporations usually receive some type of recognition for their support. This recognition, usually involving a public display of their corporate logo or a public acknowledgment of their funding, provides beneficial exposure in a community and an opportunity to position the company's brand name and logo in conjunction with some type of good deed. Examples of corporate recognition include: a company supports a running race for cancer research and places their logo on the t-shirts, another company buys a table at a fund raising event for an environmental organization and their name appears in the evening's program, another company provides a seed grant to start an arts program and receives a mention in the agency's annual report.

Most companies indicated that an acceptable and simple way for non-profit agencies to provide recognition is through display of the company's logo; although for larger grants, such as those in a capital campaign, more elaborate recognition is expected. It was stressed that non-profits should ensure the company's logo is professionally reproduced and tastefully displayed according to company guidelines. Some companies indicated an aversion to what they termed "flashy" recognition and stressed that non-profits should always contact the company for approval of any plans for displaying a corporate logo.

> **Frequent and widespread displays of a corporate logo in conjunction with a charitable agency are obviously more highly valued by the company than a single, short-term display because of the potential to reach larger numbers of consumers. Also, providing a company with sole recognition for an entire project is more highly valued than sharing recognition with other funders.**

Companies having a strategic interest in using charitable funding to obtain recognition and brand exposure tend to be those that are just beginning to experience competition in their markets, such as local phone companies and utilities, or newly merged companies seeking name recognition. Also, companies facing significant competition in consumer markets may consider recognition for their charitable funding to be a way to increase exposure of their brand and perhaps influence consumer buying decisions, or attract new customers.

Non-profits should recognize, but not over-estimate, the value of recognition to a company. With the exception of large regional or national grants, most corporate grants are small and the resultant recognition tends to be temporary and limited in scope. Frequently, only the local community or the non-profit agency's clients are aware of the company's gift, and so the recognition has only minimal impact for the company.

Also, consumers are becoming more savvy and are looking more closely at the charitable donations of corporations to determine if the donation is primarily a public relations tool, or is motivated by a real concern about an issue. Consumers are less likely to change their purchasing decisions simply because of a corporate donation to a non-profit agency. While recognition for large corporate grants, such as a capital building campaign or a national event like the Olympics, can provide significant positive exposure for a company, most recognition opportunities offered in exchange for charitable giving are seen as providing little more than limited exposure to a brand or corporate logo.

The companies I interviewed realized the basic value of recognition and said they expected non-profit agencies to offer some type of recognition for their contributions. However, all companies were quick to point out that recognition alone will not get a proposal funded and that their company's decision to fund a non-profit is not based on the agency's potential to offer some type of corporate recognition. In fact, many corporate foundation managers were not at all interested in receiving recognition for their funding. They indicated that brand recognition is the responsibility of the company's marketing department and, to some extent, the direct corporate giving program, but brand recognition is not an area of interest for the corporate foundation.

For most companies, recognition for charitable funding was simply considered a return to the company as part of a business transaction. The general feeling was that while non-profits should be able to articulate the possible recognition opportunities resulting from corporate support, their primary focus should be on explaining their programs and services.

5. Strategic Partnerships

The most often cited motivation behind corporate charitable giving was the creation of strategic partnerships between companies and non-profit agencies. The process is similar to recognition and brand exposure in that the company receives positive publicity in exchange for support of a non-profit agency. However, the recognition is not the major reason for the funding. Instead, strategic partnerships are based on a company's decision to fund those non-profits that are working on issues related to the company's core business or that match a particular business need.

Strategic partnerships are alliances of mutual interests where companies and non-profits join in pursuit of common goals. Companies seek to fund non-profit programs that are having a positive impact in an area that is linked to their corporate objectives. As one manager said,

> **"A strategic partnership is the intersection where there is benefit to the company and benefit to the community."**

Educational programs were most often listed as examples of strategic partnerships. Funding of programs to improve education was of special interest to most companies, particularly the high-tech firms, as a way of compensating for what many consider to be a public school system that inadequately prepares children for the demands of technical jobs. Companies commented that the current shortage of qualified job candidates has caused companies to compete with each other to try to hire the same qualified students.

A strategic partnership with a non-profit educational agency, therefore, would satisfy a corporate need to increase the number of skilled future employees. The shortfall of qualified employees becomes the motivation for seeking strategic partnerships with those non-profits that offer innovative, effective educational programs.

Additional examples of strategic partnerships include:

- A bank that provides loans to inner city businesses decides to support an environmental non-profit agency working to rehabilitate brownfields—vacant inner city lots that are frequently contaminated with toxins or some other environmental hazard. These brownfields are cleaned up and made more attractive to developers and potential business owners, who may then become customers of the bank when they need a loan.

- A company that sells homeowners insurance decides to fund a non-profit agency that builds low-cost housing. The company then delivers seminars on preventing losses and accidents to the non-profit's clients, which may convince the new homeowners to buy an insurance policy from the company.

- An entertainment company funds programs that develop young children's interest in the arts, in the hope of creating future customers and employees.

- A bank funds elementary school programs because of their belief that well-educated children will result in a better trained workforce, which will lead to a strong economy, which will produce a better business climate for the banking industry.

> **In these strategic partnerships, the corporate charitable funding was not based on altruistic motives, but instead on a desire to advance a business goal. Although the process involved some type of charitable giving, the ultimate result was improvement of some aspect of the corporation's business.**

Understanding what a company is trying to accomplish with its charitable giving program allows the non-profit agency to emphasize the match between their programs and the company's strategic interests. The importance of identifying this linkage was evident in the responses of the corporate managers to the questionnaire. (See Figure 2.2.)

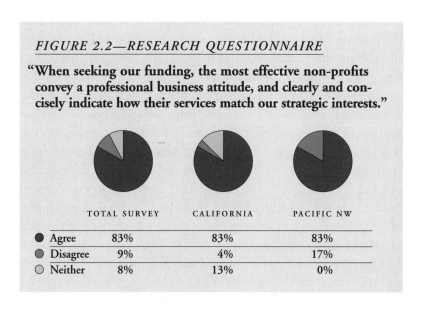

FIGURE 2.2—RESEARCH QUESTIONNAIRE

"When seeking our funding, the most effective non-profits convey a professional business attitude, and clearly and concisely indicate how their services match our strategic interests."

	TOTAL SURVEY	CALIFORNIA	PACIFIC NW
● Agree	83%	83%	83%
● Disagree	9%	4%	17%
○ Neither	8%	13%	0%

These responses also reinforce the professional tone of the entire corporate funding process. For your funding request to be seriously considered by a corporation, you must ensure that all your interactions with corporations positively reflect the strength and capability of your agency. You may be hoping to convey your financial need or your simple grassroots nature by submitting a poorly conceived or hastily composed package; but instead, you may create the perception that your agency is unprofessional or incompetent and, therefore, a poor investment choice for the company.

☞ Corporate Philanthropy as a Business Transaction

Corporate philanthropy is best compared to a business transaction since there are benefits for both the corporation and the non-profit. Corporate charitable support, as we have seen, meets a company's strategic interest, while also providing non-profits with much needed financial support. Attracting corporate funding also allows the non-profit agency to use the good reputation of the company to validate the effectiveness of its programs and perhaps attract funding from other corporations.

However beneficial it may appear, this transaction with a corporation should not to be entered without some deliberation by the non-profit. You must be conscious of the fact that accepting support from a corporation, even in the form of a small-sized grant, links your agency's name to the company, its reputation, its business practices, to the quality of its products and even to the types of products or services the company provides. The public's perception of your agency can be critically impacted by both the positive and negative perceptions of a company. The unpopular actions taken by a corporation, actions which you may not know about and which you may not support, can reflect badly on your agency. Your agency's willingness to accept money from a company could be interpreted as approval of its actions and cause your donors and advocates to quickly drop their support of your agency in favor of another.

Your advocates might not even need a questionable corporate activity to cause them to withdraw their support of your programs. The business in which a company engages or the products that it produces may be reason enough to cause your supporters to flee. Non-profits have been known to lose the support of donors who felt the non-profit compromised its integrity by accepting corporate funds.

While you cannot predict corporate direction, you can get an idea of a company's culture and the value system motivating its actions by talking with current and past employees and scanning the business section of the newspaper. You can use the library or Internet to research a company and identify any past or present incidents, or business practices that you may consider inappropriate, unethical, illegal or in opposition to your agency's mission. You can also carefully review the product line and services produced by a company to determine if your agency's support of these products is a violation of its mission. Failure to research a company's history and business practices, and failure to evaluate the consequences of accepting a company's support, may forever link your agency's reputation with a tarnished corporate reputation and irreparably damage your agency's ability to effectively work in the community.

☞ Implications and Recommendations

- Before beginning a search for corporate support, consider developing corporate funding policies, approved by your Board of Directors, which define:

  - the industries and companies you will and will not approach for funding.

  - the limits of the recognition you will offer to corporations.

  - the boundaries around any partnership you form with a corporation.

- Become aware of the companies that do business in your geographic area, since they will be most interested in funding your programs. Read the newspaper daily, or if your time is limited, at least skim the business pages and the front page of the local newspaper each day, looking for articles describing corporate activities. Be aware of any controversy that might cause you to avoid the company. Look for announcements of the opening of local branches since these companies will be looking for acceptance into the community, perhaps by funding or providing volunteers for your agency. Also, look for articles describing any new company interest that might be related to your mission. Target these companies for further research.

- Requests for corporate funding and all communications with the company (phone calls, letters, etc.) should portray your agency as a strong, successful organization and an attractive candidate for investment. There is no need to feel intimidated because you work for a non-profit agency or because your budget is small. You are doing great things! Your work is critically needed in our society! Focus on your successes. Demonstrate a pride in your accomplishments and recognize the importance of your work to the community and to the company.

- Companies want to support winners. Do not tell a company you will close your doors if you do not receive their grant. (Even if it's true.) Instead, explain your agency's achievements and focus on your positive results. Present yourself as a successful agency that is now seeking the company's support in order to continue or expand the improvements you have made in the community. I am not suggesting that you should intentionally misrepresent your financial situation. You can explain your financial status in the budget section of your proposal. (See Chapter 7 for a discussion of budgets.) But your focus should be on the positive aspects of your agency.

- Market your agency as a good investment. Remember that only a few corporate funders are motivated by altruism, but all companies want to invest in something successful. The more you can communicate how you will be successful, the more likely you will be to attract a funder.

- Remember to portray a professional image in all your interactions. Professionalism does not mean spending lots of money on fancy materials. Professionalism is an attitude, a way of conducting business that communicates the capability of your staff and agency.

- List any influential connections you may have, but do not expect personal connections alone to compensate for a poorly prepared proposal.

- Offer recognition opportunities in exchange for funding, but do not make the recognition the focal point of your presentation. Remember that recognition is the by-product of your business relationship with the company. Devote most of your time to developing a strong case for your request.

- Identify which donors, volunteers and clients work for a company with a matching gifts program. Periodically recheck for anyone who may have switched employers or companies that may have added matching gift programs.

- Understand how you fit with the company's strategic interests, but focus on presenting a compelling case. Let the company determine how well you fit their interests.

CHAPTER 3
Understanding the Funding Process

☞ How Companies Select Areas for Funding

Like most private foundations, corporations target their charitable funding to specific issues and/or geographic locations. They seek to support projects that will leverage their funding and give them the most visibility for their dollar, and so they target those issues they feel most able to impact. There is a growing reluctance among companies to join in funding the current popular cause. Some refuse to fund what they termed "the disease of the year" because of a concern that their support will be lost amid the crowd of funders or overshadowed by larger gifts. Instead, the companies want their charitable giving to distinguish their company in some way and set it apart from other funders.

Corporate managers frequently cited non-profit agencies with "demonstrated impact and sustainability" as being most likely to receive their funding. Impact was defined as "an ability to create measurable change in the community," and sustainability was defined as "an ability to obtain financial support, over the long term, from a variety of different sources." Companies generally want to support strong non-profit agencies, and not those that are on the brink of bankruptcy or looking for help to pay off debt. Corporations, as a rule, tend to be "risk-adverse" and this is generally reflected in their funding program. Dollars are generally directed toward less controversial issues and there is a reluctance to fund any issues that might alienate shareholders or customers.

A few companies did indicate a willingness to consider supporting non-profit agencies that dealt with controversial issues, hoping that their support would be the catalyst that raises awareness of the issue and attracts additional corporate funders. In order to be funded, however, it was felt that the controversy must be related to an issue of importance to the community. Conflict for its own sake was not considered of interest to any company.

☞ The Importance of Guidelines

The specific areas and issues each corporation funds are listed in their guidelines and reading these guidelines is a necessary first step to obtaining corporate funding. However, just reading the guidelines is not sufficient. As one manager said,

> **"You must believe the guidelines. Do not try to force a match between your program and a corporation's guidelines."**

Since corporations cannot possibly fund all the worthy issues and all the worthy requests, guidelines allow companies to set boundaries around their charitable giving, making their philanthropic program more manageable and related to their business goals. As a non-profit, you may believe your issue is urgent, it may be important to the community, it may even be something you **think** the company should fund, but unless it's listed in the company's guidelines, your request will not be considered. Most managers said they do not even read proposals that do not fit their guidelines.

> **Companies reported that 40% to 90% of the proposals received each year are immediately rejected because they do not fit the targeted funding areas or geographic areas defined in their guidelines.**

Many of the corporate representatives reported that non-profit agencies sometimes try to convince them to fund an issue that is beyond the scope of their corporation's giving program. However, attempting to force a manager to consider a proposal that clearly does not meet the company's guidelines is an ineffective tactic.

Staff managers rarely have the authority to unilaterally change a corporation's targeted funding areas. Also, your actions might create a negative perception of your agency and perhaps damage your future requests for funding. (As one manager said, "We have long memories.")

In addition, it is important to realize that many corporate foundation managers periodically communicate with each other. Intentionally alienating one company representative could damage your agency's reputation with others in the corporate funding community. Just accept the fact that you do not match the funding program of this particular company and move on to another company.

☞ Categories of Corporate Funding

Corporate funding can be divided into two categories: broad industry-related issues and smaller community-related issues. Some companies have programs that are a combination of both categories. The issues funded and the size of grants frequently differ by category. The following is a list of additional characteristics of each category:

1. Industry-Related Funding

- The areas targeted for funding are usually defined by the CEO, corporation executives or the corporate foundation's trustees based upon their beliefs about the most critical issues. Funding is given to those issues that are closely related to the core business and company objectives. The projects and agencies that are funded generally involve statewide or national issues.

- These grants are generally large in size ($20,000 and larger) and proposals are expected to be more sophisticated. There are specific due dates and decisions are frequently made at quarterly board meetings, although some boards meet only once a year. Funding decisions may take from 6 to 12 months, or longer.

- Modifications in funding are primarily influenced by changes in the corporate culture and the company objectives, or shifts in the perception of the company's senior executives or board trustees. For example, a bank originally funds college level education, but their growing belief that children are unprepared for the rigors of college studies causes them to shift their funding to K-12 educational programs. Similarly, a computer firm initially funds programs that introduce technology to the public, but as computers become more ubiquitous, they shift funding to programs that demonstrate new uses for computer technology.

- The corporate foundation's trustees or executive managers set policy and direction. The foundation staff functions as advisors to the decision-makers—researching non-profit agencies and issues and making recommendations. Foundation staff managers usually do not have decision-making authority, or have limited authority to approve grants only to a certain monetary level. There usually is minimal or very limited input from local employees in the decision-making process.

2. Community-Related Funding

- The issues targeted for community-related funding may differ from the company's industry-related funding goals. Funding is generally given to agencies that meet the needs of the communities where employees live and work.

- Funding areas may change frequently in response to changing community needs.

- Grants are usually smaller than industry-related grants and proposal requirements are less stringent.

- Sponsorship of special events is more prevalent and funding may come from the budget of the local marketing department which is likely to be interested in opportunities for displaying the company logo in exchange for financial support.

- Employee involvement in the non-profit agency is valued, and having employees as volunteers can positively impact a non-profit agency's proposal.

- Employee input to the decision-making process is more prevalent, although the degree of employee involvement varies among companies. Companies with widespread rural constituencies tend to rely on local employees to a greater extent, particularly when identifying and prioritizing the community needs that will be targeted for funding. As staff budgets continue to be reduced, local employees are being given more input to the funding decision and are sometimes asked to make site-visits to determine an agency's effectiveness, or evaluate the outcomes of a project that has been funded.

☞ # Insight into the Decision Making Process

Although some differences do exist among companies, there are similarities in the process of reviewing proposals across all the companies I interviewed. Most utilize some form of pre-screening, such as requiring a letter of intent or a phone call, to eliminate proposals that do not meet their guidelines or their geographic limitations. Also, many companies process community proposals differently than industry-related proposals.

1. Deciding to fund industry-related grants.

Large statewide or multi-state industry proposals are usually sent to the company's headquarters where the foundation staff performs the initial screen of the proposal, researches the agency and the program, conducts site-visits and sends funding recommendations to the executive level staff or the board trustees who make the final funding decision.

Although they may not make the actual funding decision, the foundation staff members' opinions about proposals and individual non-profit agencies are often highly valued by the corporate decision-makers, and frequently influence the final decision. Some companies allow staff members to make decisions to fund proposals up to a certain monetary amount, allowing the trustees and executives to focus on proposals requesting larger amounts.

> **The proposal document that you submit to the company is not always seen by the decision-makers.**

Due to the high volume of proposals received each year, the staff of many corporate foundations are required to summarize each proposal before presenting it to the decision-makers. Frequently, individual proposals are reduced to a single page or even less. The funding decisions are based on these summaries, together with staff recommendations, and not on the complete document you originally submitted.

In other companies, the proposals are divided among the foundation board members. These board members read and review only the proposals they were assigned, and then make recommendations to the entire group. Funding is decided by the entire board based on a discussion of these recommendations, and not on a discussion of the actual document you submitted. For these reasons, it is important to learn to write a proposal that communicates your program in a clear and concise manner.

> **Submitting a proposal that communicates your salient points in a few paragraphs increases the potential that your own words, rather than a staff member's interpretation of your words, will become part of the summary sent to the corporate decision-makers.**

2. Deciding to fund community grants.

The process of funding smaller community projects, in most companies, generally involves some involvement or input from the local branch manager, company representative or employees. The extent of local employee involvement, however, varies among companies. Some companies require that community proposals be submitted directly to local managers who are considered to be most aware of local issues. This is particularly true for companies that service rural geographies, since it is considered impossible for headquarters staff to remain current on all issues relevant to these local constituencies. The locally submitted proposals are quickly reviewed and decisions are made with little or no headquarters staff input.

Companies serving urban areas, or a combination of both rural and urban areas, usually require that community-related proposals be sent to headquarters staff for a decision, although the local company representatives may be asked for input. A variation used by a few companies involves the headquarters staff providing only a recommendation, while the local company representatives make the final decision.

Regardless of the internal process used by a particular company, it is important to realize that your proposal may be read by a number of people, all with limited time and limited knowledge of your agency. Be certain to submit a clear and concise proposal. Do not be too concerned with identifying the type of decision-making process that a company may use, instead focus on following the company's requirements for submission of proposals.

> **In all communications with a corporation, be clear, stay with the facts and avoid long emotional pleas.**

You should also realize that most of these corporate decision-making processes take quite a bit of time. Despite the urgency of your need for the funds, not any amount of pressure on the staff, nor an avalanche of phone calls, will speed up the decision. There is a need, therefore, for advance planning on the part of non-profits seeking corporate support. Proposals must not only meet the company's published deadline, but they also must be submitted early enough to ensure a decision will have been made before the project begins and the funds are needed. Check the company's guidelines for specific details regarding the length of time required for their funding decision.

☞ Employee Committees and the Funding Decision

Many companies involve employees in the funding process and decisions made by teams of employees are common. These employees frequently volunteer for this position and undertake the work in addition to their regular jobs. Involving employees in the funding process compensates for smaller staff sizes by assigning the employees some of the tasks normally performed by the foundation staff.

Some companies, with employees spread throughout large rural geographic areas, have assigned the actual decision-making authority for small grants to local employee teams. This is based on a belief that employees living and working in the area are not only aware of the most critical community needs, they also know which non-profit agencies are most effectively addressing those needs. In addition, many employees work as volunteers or board members for these non-profit agencies and have "insider information" about the viability of the agency, the skill level of its leaders and the agency's ability to carry on its programs into the future.

If you are seeking corporate funding for a local community program, take advantage of this practice of involving employees in funding decisions. The local employees can become your gateway into the company by recommending your program to the corporate foundation staff, educating you about the corporate culture and the company's business goals, and informing you of changes to the company's funding policies. This information can play a critical role in helping to align your proposal with corporate interests.

Consider introducing the local company employees, particularly the management employees, to your programs. While many companies involve both managers and hourly employees in the funding process, it is generally felt that managers are more knowledgeable of the company's long-term strategic direction and can more effectively identify which non-profit agencies match their corporate interests.

Before you begin to write the proposal, try to schedule a meeting with the company's local branch manager or store manager to introduce your program and its impact in the community. Encourage employee involvement, and offer volunteer projects that could serve as team-building opportunities for company employees. Managers frequently look for innovative ways to increase morale among the employees, and volunteer projects can provide this opportunity. Present your volunteer project as a way to increase the company's visibility in the community, another area of interest for local managers.

Tell the local manager of your plans to submit a proposal and request her support. After the funding decision has been made, call the manager and thank her for supporting your proposal, even if your request was denied. This will create a favorable impression with the manager and could be advantageous in the event you decide to reapply for funding at a later date.

In your efforts to cultivate relationships with local employees, take care not to circumvent the guidelines. Always mail your proposal to the address listed in the guidelines. Do not send the proposal to the local manager unless instructed to do so by the guidelines. If local employees advise you to follow a proposal format that differs from the published guidelines, check the accuracy of that information with the corporate staff before proceeding. The employee who advised you to submit a proposal may have been trying to be helpful, but he may not have been aware of the new guideline requirements. Remember, you must **believe the company's guidelines!**

☞ ## The Impact of Staff Reductions on the Decision-Making Process

The competitive nature of the marketplace requires most companies to continually look for ways to reduce their cost of doing business. Despite seemingly large profits, very few companies in the past few years have been able to avoid the need to reduce or reallocate their operating budgets. These budget cuts and resultant employee reductions affect all departments, but tend to impact staff functions, including the corporate foundation staff, to a greater extent. The companies I interviewed were no different. Most had been hard hit by "downsizing" and reported corporate foundation staff reductions of 25% to 75% during the past five years.

Anyone who has worked in a corporation knows that regardless of the size of staff reductions, the workload usually remains the same. Most corporate foundation staffs are responsible for the same amount of work today as five years ago, but with fewer employees. Their workload may even be growing larger as more non-profits submit corporate proposals in an attempt to replace reductions in government funding. Some managers reported receiving thousands of proposals a year!

In addition, many managers, particularly those responsible for the direct corporate giving programs, are responsible for more than just charitable contributions. Employee relations, volunteer programs, United Way and retiree programs are just some of the additional duties of many of these managers.

The size and scope of the corporate manager's job is an important point for non-profit agencies to keep in mind. Any interaction you may have with a corporation—a phone call, a letter of inquiry or a full proposal—should be clear, concise and reflect a value for the manager's time. If you cannot communicate your major points on the phone in two or three sentences, or on paper in the first paragraph, stop and reformat your thoughts or you risk losing the manager's interest.

☞ Funding of Start-Up vs. Established Non-Profit Agencies

During the interviews, I was interested in corporations' opinions of newly formed, "start-up" non-profit agencies and asked a number of questions pertaining to this issue. In response to my questions, almost all the companies were skeptical of the need for the creation of completely new non-profit agencies. The following comment was representative of the feelings of most companies:

> **"There are so many non-profits already in existence, it's unlikely an idea is not already being tried elsewhere. Why start a new agency; why not add to an existing one?"**

The fact that a newly established non-profit agency plans to be involved in doing something "good" in the community is not reason enough, in the opinion of the corporate representatives, to start-up a completely new non-profit agency. There must also be a verifiable need in the community that is not already being addressed by established non-profits.

In addition to questioning the need for the creation of new non-profits, many companies also expressed a reluctance to provide financial support to these new agencies. This is primarily because most companies consider their charitable giving to be an investment in the community, and like other financial investments, funding is not directed toward any project that appears risky or untested. Lacking a track record of accomplishments, start-up non-profit agencies are generally considered to be too great a risk for corporate investment. Corporations want to support "winners" and it's easier to identify "winners" among established non-profit agencies. As one manager said,

> **"We support established non-profit groups because there are too many start-ups out there, and they are in competition for the same population and the same geography. There is no way to judge if a start-up non-profit will be successful."**

Most corporations prefer to fund new non-profits only after they have been in existence for a few years and can demonstrate a measurable impact in the community. A lack of time prevents most companies from completing detailed research of newly formed non-profits and their programs. Therefore, even a potentially excellent program from a new non-profit agency will most probably be considered risky and will have difficulty attracting corporate support during its first few years of operation.

Corporations want to fund programs that have proven to be effective and that appear to have the necessary strength to survive into the future. Companies believe these characteristics are easier to identify in a non-profit with an established track record. Established non-profit agencies are also the preferred funding candidates because, over the years, they usually have acquired a broad base of support in the community and are attractive to a company seeking linkage to a well-respected non-profit.

If you are an established non-profit agency, your chances of receiving corporate funding may be a little stronger than a start-up agency, but not guaranteed. In fact, corporations indicated a growing concern that some established non-profits are becoming less effective as the years pass. There is a belief that many established non-profit agencies are becoming too bureaucratic, have increasingly high overhead costs and are unresponsive to the changing needs of a rapidly changing world.

In order to attract corporate support, established non-profit agencies must continue to demonstrate positive results. Corporations, like other funders, will not support a non-profit agency simply because of its past reputation or previous achievements. As one manager said,

> **"You can't just depend on the fact that you are a well-known charity. There are lots of well-known groups out there looking for the same dollars."**

Established non-profit agencies must keep connected to their community and clientele so that they will be able to recognize subtle shifts in the clients' needs. Then, the agency must also be astute enough and willing enough to modify its mission, if needed, to meet the changing needs of their population. Remember, corporations want to make an impact in the community; they want to support real solutions to current problems. As a non-profit, you must be certain you are requesting funding for a program that is meeting a present need and not a need that existed ten years ago.

Modifying your agency's mission is not something a non-profit should undertake casually. It should not be considered without first surveying the community and understanding the needs of your clientele. Changes in an agency's programs or overall direction, based solely on intuition or assumptions, are just as dangerous as changing your mission in order to fit a corporation's funding guidelines. Changes in mission should not occur very often and should be done only in response to **significant** changes in the needs of the community. Thoughtful shifts in your mission and program goals to meet changes in community needs are indicative of a client-centered agency—an attribute attractive to many companies.

Examples of changes in the community which might indicate a need for appropriate modifications to an established agency's mission include situations such as:

- An inner city health care agency recognizes the changing demographics of their community and sees a need to begin to offer bilingual programs, or augment existing bilingual programs with additional languages.

- A daycare agency expands its hours to late night and early morning hours to meet parents' changing work schedules. Perhaps they even expand into daycare for seniors.

☞ ## Suggestions for New Agencies Seeking Corporate Funding

Although it was evident from my interviews that new non-profit agencies have special hurdles to overcome if they are to obtain corporate support, it is not impossible. The following suggestions are designed to assist new agencies begin to attract the interest of corporate funders:

1. Demonstrate uniqueness.

Funding requests from start-up agencies are not automatically rejected by corporations, but in order to attract corporate support, new agencies must demonstrate a uniqueness. They must articulate the value they add to the community and the unique role of their service within the network of existing services. As one manager said,

> "A new non-profit needs to be more than someone's good idea. There must be a need in the community that the agency will fill, a need that is not being filled elsewhere."

If your service or program is not unique in the community and other similar agencies already exist, you must show the need for adding your agency. The following are suggested ways to demonstrate this need:

- Define the scope of the problem. Use quantifiable facts to demonstrate that the need for your service exceeds existing community resources. For example, in many major cities the need for additional homeless shelters can easily be documented by comparing the number of homeless individuals with the number of available beds.

- Indicate the way in which your agency will complement existing agencies in the community. For example, your agency might offer child care service on weekends, holidays and at night, while existing child care agencies offer these service only during regular working hours.

- Explain the way in which your agency will do the same job more effectively than existing agencies. For example, your program might provide comparable services to more clients, and at a lower cost than the services currently provided. Use quantifiable facts to illustrate your case, but do not make disparaging comments about existing service providers.

2. Demonstrate strong leadership.

New non-profits seeking corporate funding must also be viewed as strong organizations. High-quality leadership, both on the staff and on the board, is one indicator of organizational strength that is valued by companies.

For many companies, a decision to invest in a small start-up non-profit, too new to generate proven results, was viewed as a decision to invest in the skill and reputation of its Executive Director. Companies, particularly in the Pacific Northwest, were more comfortable supporting a new agency if the Executive Director was known as a strong and capable leader.

A new agency led by an experienced, effective Executive Director could overcome a company's reluctance to support start-up agencies. Some companies even indicated a willingness to consider funding a start-up agency solely on the basis of their previous interactions with the Executive Director. Less well-known Executive Directors need to emphasize their skill and capability for the position.

3. Demonstrate fiscal strength.

Companies believe that a new non-profit agency's organizational strength is also reflected, to some degree, in its financials. Strong financial statements and well-planned budgets can boost the credibility of new agencies seeking corporate support. Newly formed agencies should seek the services of an accountant or a volunteer skilled in non-profit finances to assist with the development of an accurate budget and financial statements.

A new agency's financial stability is also enhanced by including a list of other funders in the proposal. This list should be more than a "wish list" and should consist of actual, committed funding sources for your program. A small corporate grant will not ensure sustainability for your programs, and so companies want to see that your agency has obtained the funds needed for the ongoing operation of its programs. In fact, start-up non-profits have a better chance of obtaining corporate funding if their proposal is submitted after they have already obtained funding from other sources.

4. Submitting background material—a word of caution.

Start-up non-profit agencies sometimes send background information about their organization to corporations before submitting a proposal, in order to create an awareness of their work. The expectation is that the proposal will be received more favorably if the corporation first receives material introducing the non-profit and its programs. Yet, when I asked companies about the effectiveness of this practice, only about 40% agreed with the process. (See Figure 3.1.)

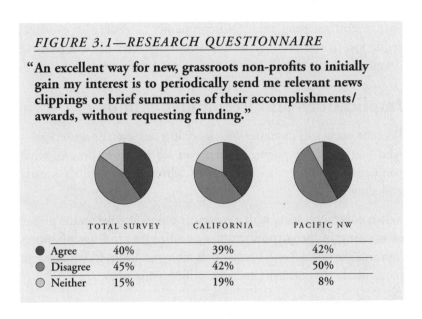

FIGURE 3.1—RESEARCH QUESTIONNAIRE

"An excellent way for new, grassroots non-profits to initially gain my interest is to periodically send me relevant news clippings or brief summaries of their accomplishments/ awards, without requesting funding."

		TOTAL SURVEY	CALIFORNIA	PACIFIC NW
●	Agree	40%	39%	42%
●	Disagree	45%	42%	50%
○	Neither	15%	19%	8%

The results were a bit surprising since I expected more managers to disapprove of the practice because of the constraints on their time. Still, since less than half of the responses were positive, I would not suggest sending unsolicited background material to a corporate foundation staff as a way of introducing your agency.

While introducing your program to **local company managers** and encouraging employees to become volunteers can increase the attractiveness of your proposal, be aware that unsolicited material sent to the **corporate foundation staff** will probably be lost in the mass of paperwork received by these managers each day. It is more effective and less time consuming to follow the company's published guidelines and submit only the requested information with your proposal or letter of inquiry.

Before ending this discussion of start-up and established non-profits, it is important to understand that most companies expect that continued reductions in government funding will have dramatic repercussions on the entire non-profit sector in the years ahead. The companies believe that ineffective, established non-profit agencies, as well as start-up non-profit agencies that are just replicating existing programs, will be unable to compete for sufficient funding and will cease to exist, while their clients will move to another agency with a stronger program. Most companies consider this eventual reduction in the number of non-profit agencies to be a positive development in the evolution of the non-profit sector.

☞ Implications and Recommendations

- Become proficient in telling your story in a few, concise sentences— who you are, your purpose, what you are trying to do and what you need from the company. Practice delivering your "pitch" clearly and slowly.

- When communicating with a company representative on the phone or meeting in the corporate offices, realize that feelings of apprehension are normal and usually pass after you begin the discussion, particularly if you have practiced telling your story.

- Be able to respond clearly and concisely to questions about your project. Keep notes nearby in the event you receive a phone call asking for an explanation of something in the proposal. Circulate your proposal around your office; let others know it's been sent and prepare them to respond to questions, in the event a funder calls when you are not available.

- Recognize that your proposal may be read on a plane by a tired manager after a long day, or it may be read by a volunteer during a lunch break, or it may be summarized before it even gets to the decision-maker. Be certain your proposal is clear, concise and readable.

- Regardless of your agency's size or years of experience, look for ways to increase the visibility of your agency in the community. Market your agency and its mission at local business networking functions, such as meetings of the Chamber of Commerce. Get to know the local representatives of the companies you are targeting for support and try to interest their employees in volunteer opportunities. Local representatives, at the very least, may provide a helpful recommendation for your program.

- Recognize that corporations are more than just large, imposing structures. Corporations are made up of people, just like you or me, and they have good days and bad days, just like you or me. Remember to be patient and, in all of your interactions, treat the company representatives the same way you would like to be treated.

- There are a lot of good ideas out there, but not every good idea fills a need in the community. Before creating a new non-profit agency, investigate the resources currently available in the community. Honestly answer the questions, "Is there a real need for starting this new non-profit? Can existing resources satisfy the need instead?"

- Periodically, re-evaluate your agency's impact in the community. Be alert for changes in your clientele or in the community, and be willing to consider modifications to your mission as your clients and their needs change. Never change your mission simply to match company guidelines or available funding opportunities.

- Do not try to prove your uniqueness by criticizing other agencies. Instead, emphasize your distinctiveness and the value you will add to existing community services. Know the work of your competition, be able to articulate the similarities and differences and how you complement their work.

- Although some companies are willing to fund start-up agencies, generally, new non-profits should not expect corporations to satisfy their funding needs. For the first few years of operation, new agencies should plan on raising the majority of their funds from other sources, such as private foundations and individual donors.

CHAPTER 4
The Role of Personal Connections

☞ Misconceptions About the Importance of Personal Connections

The role of personal connections is one of the most misunderstood aspects of corporate funding. Many non-profits mistakenly believe that corporate funding decisions are based solely on "who you know," and only those non-profit agencies whose board members regularly golf with a corporation's CEO can successfully attract corporate support. My research indicates that this is not the case.

Although funding of a particular non-profit agency can be enhanced through a personal friendship with a corporate executive, funding based entirely on friendships or on some other type of personal relationship happens much less frequently than you might think. Personal relationships and friendships with corporate executives are not critical to the funding process, and friendships alone will not win corporate support for programs that are outside the boundaries of the corporate funding area. Non-profit agencies that meet company guidelines should not hesitate to pursue corporate support simply because they have no personal friendships within a company.

In the interviews, most corporate representatives felt that the strongest relationships between corporations and non-profits begin after funding has been approved and the non-profit starts to achieve results because of the company's support. This relationship frequently grows stronger as the non-profit continues to demonstrate an ability to use corporate funding to positively impact the community.

As an example, one company described a relationship that began when a non-profit received a small grant for its programs serving the physically disabled. Impressed with the results, the company funded the program the following year. Over the next few years, a personal connection was created as the staff of the corporation and the staff of the non-profit met periodically and had frequent phone discussions about the program. Corporate support expanded to include donations of equipment, as well as employee volunteers. After more then a decade of connection, now the company not only continues to provide financial support, but also has helped the non-profit agency develop new programs.

☞ Cultivating a Connection Within a Company

While the success of your proposal is not dependent on who you know in a company, some type of connection can be advantageous and help your proposal stand out amid the crowd of other proposals that are requesting the same corporate funding.

Taking the time to research and identify connections to a company is not difficult nor does it take much time. Many non-profits, however, still consider it easier to simply address the envelope and mail the proposal to all the companies in the area, hoping that at least one company will be interested. This approach may seem easier, but mass mailings are not particularly effective. Remember your proposal is competing with hundreds, and in some cases, thousands of other proposals, all from respected non-profits doing important work in the community. Your proposal will have a better chance of being funded if you spend some time identifying someone working in the company who is also affiliated, in some way, with your agency. Identifying that connection is not as difficult as it initially seems.

You do not need to know the CEO on a first name basis, or join the same country club as the company president, or have lunch with the Chairman of the Corporate Board. The most common methods of connecting with a corporation involve linkages with corporate employees. Corporate employees may be your donors, volunteers or even your clients. Spending the time to research your membership and clientele for names of corporate employees, before submitting a proposal, will improve the reception your proposal eventually receives.

☞ Making a Connection Through Employees

Employees can provide a connection to a company by supplying background information about the company and also by functioning as a reference, certifying the capability and impact of the non-profit applying for the grant. Employees can assist with research of a company's funding program and inform you of any internal company changes that might affect the company's future funding strategies. Employees can explain the corporate culture and help determine how your programs might fit with the funding interests of the company. They can provide contact information and perhaps even introduce you to the foundation managers.

A company's local managers are sometimes asked by the corporate foundation for input about the effectiveness of an agency. Cultivating a relationship with managers of local stores, branches or company offices, and increasing their awareness or involvement with your programs, can add to the credibility of your proposal. This is particularly true for companies with branches or offices dispersed over wide geographic regions, or in primarily rural areas. The corporate foundation managers in these areas cannot possibly become familiar with all the non-profit agencies in a widespread geography, and so they depend on the input of local employees to verify the material in a proposal and confirm the effectiveness of a non-profit agency seeking the company's support.

During my interviews, a number of company representatives suggested that developing a personal relationship with their employees or local company managers is an effective way to begin the process of seeking corporate funds. (See Figure 4.1.)

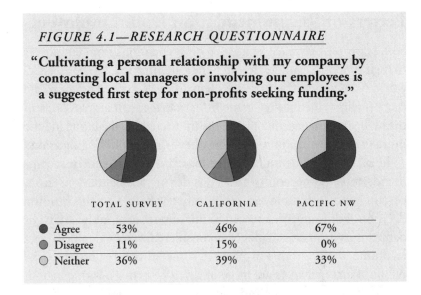

FIGURE 4.1—RESEARCH QUESTIONNAIRE

"Cultivating a personal relationship with my company by contacting local managers or involving our employees is a suggested first step for non-profits seeking funding."

		TOTAL SURVEY	CALIFORNIA	PACIFIC NW
●	Agree	53%	46%	67%
●	Disagree	11%	15%	0%
○	Neither	36%	39%	33%

These figures indicate that cultivation of a personal relationship with **local** company representatives is most important for non-profits seeking corporate funding in the Pacific Northwest. This may be due to the widespread rural geography and their need to rely on the input from local employees to supplement the corporate foundation staffs' knowledge of local non-profits. In addition, there is a "small town" feel to even the largest cities in the Pacific Northwest which, more so than in California, offers an opportunity for members of the funding community to establish relationships with the non-profit agencies. As one manager in the Pacific Northwest said, "We all see each other in the grocery store and at the gym, and we know each other." This informal contact adds to the corporation's familiarity with the non-profit agency and their awareness of the non-profit's work, and decreases the risk that many corporations associate with funding unknown non-profit agencies.

☞ Letters of Recommendation from Employees

Some non-profits attach written recommendations from employees to their proposals, and my research indicates that this can be an effective way to connect with some companies. Recommendations are more highly valued if they come from management employees, and the higher the management level, the more credible the input and the more impact the recommendations have on the funding decision.

In addition to the higher value placed on management recommendations, some companies consider recommendations from certain types of employees to be more valuable to the funding decision. For example, a recommendation from a public affairs or community relations manager is considered more valuable than a recommendation from a manager in some other function, since the public affairs managers are more likely to be better informed about the business motivations and priorities of the company's charitable funding. It is important to remember that a recommendation from an employee or from the local company representative is helpful, but again, it is not a guarantee of funding.

It should be noted that a few companies indicated that letters of recommendation from local employees were of no advantage to the non-profit seeking funding since the local company representatives frequently were unaware of the corporate strategic direction and funding priorities.

Unless the guidelines discourage it, a **few** letters of recommendation generally add to the credibility of your proposal, but too many letters can be overwhelming and can detract from the effectiveness of your proposal. If a company employee is a volunteer or client of your agency, ask them for a letter of recommendation and attach it to your proposal, or ask that the recommendation be sent via the company's e-mail. The recommendation will help distinguish your proposal from the others, but it will not guarantee funding. Your agency must still meet the company's guidelines and present its case more effectively than the other non-profit agencies that are also requesting funding.

☞ Attracting Employees as Volunteers

If your agency currently has no volunteers from local companies, seeking out corporate volunteers can help future fund raising efforts. However, attracting the interest of corporate employees is not always easy. Frequently, employees are trying to juggle work and family responsibilities, and feel unable to volunteer any time to charitable causes. Their reluctance to volunteer is not the result of a lack of interest in community affairs. Instead, the demands of work and family leave corporate employees with little time to learn about the critical issues in their community and the importance of the work done by local non-profit agencies.

If you are to successfully entice employees to carve out time from their busy schedules to volunteer with your agency, you must develop their awareness of the good work done by your agency and the need for an agency of your type. You must find a way to educate employees about what you do and why your work is needed. You must also find a way to excite them about your work. This may require a little planning. It will definitely require some creativity. You will need to do more than just post flyers or mail volunteer meeting announcements. You must also look for unique opportunities to market your agency to corporate employees.

A very effective and exciting way to demonstrate your value in the community is by demonstrating to employees the service you provide. Contact the public relations office of a large company or the manager of a local company, introduce your agency and ask for permission to demonstrate your services on company premises for a day or even a week. The following are examples of techniques for attracting the interest of corporate volunteers.

Techniques to Attract Corporate Volunteers

- If you are an organization that teaches music or dance to children, offer to entertain employees in the company lobby at lunch time.

- If you are an arts agency, offer to exhibit the work of your clients in an employee break room.

- If you are a family counseling agency, offer a day of free on-the-job counseling to employees who are concerned about their children.

- If you are an environmental agency, offer a free seminar on how to reduce electricity usage in the home, or offer to advise an employee committee about beginning a company recycling program.

- If you are a health care agency, offer free blood pressure screening in the company lobby.

If employees can see, hear and experience your work, they are more likely to consider volunteering their services. You might even attract the attention and interest of the corporate foundation manager. Once employees begin volunteering, keep in close contact with them. Ask the employees to request a copy of the company's annual report from their public affairs department, and discuss with the employees their understanding of the company's goals and future plans. These discussions may provide clues about the company's future funding interests. Remember to also ask if the company offers a matching gift program.

☞ Employees as Board Members

Involving employees in leadership roles in your agency is another way to connect with a company. Playing golf with a company's executive will probably have very little impact on your chances of being funded by that company, but having that same executive serve as a member of your Board of Directors can significantly increase your chances of obtaining funding.

Most companies consider the input of all employee volunteers when evaluating the proposal of a non-profit, but they tend to place more weight on the recommendations of those employees who serve on the non-profit's Board of Directors. The Board of Directors position is seen as requiring more of a commitment and is, therefore, considered a more credible indicator of the employee's true feeling toward the agency and its work.

But before you go out and change the makeup of your board, you should know that the composition of Boards of Directors, although important, is not necessarily a significant factor in the funding decisions of companies. A corporate executive serving as a board member will give your proposal a distinct advantage, but it will not guarantee funding. Only about one-third of the company representatives indicated that a board composed of influential members affected their funding decision. (See Figure 4.2.)

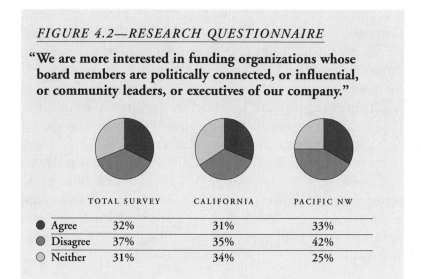

FIGURE 4.2—RESEARCH QUESTIONNAIRE

"We are more interested in funding organizations whose board members are politically connected, or influential, or community leaders, or executives of our company."

		TOTAL SURVEY	CALIFORNIA	PACIFIC NW
●	Agree	32%	31%	33%
◑	Disagree	37%	35%	42%
○	Neither	31%	34%	25%

Responses to this question were consistent across geographic regions. A few companies indicated they definitely would fund any non-profit where their executive served as a board member in order to encourage the executive's involvement in the community and increase good will among potential customers. However, most other companies indicated that funding was likely if one of their executives served on a non-profit's Board of Directors at the request of the company and officially represented the company. However, if the executive's board membership was purely the result of a personal interest, funding would not be assured.

☞ ## Connecting Through Purchase of a Company's Products

Although development of relationships with local employees can help your proposal, using the company's products or services will most likely have no impact at all. Including, in your proposal, statements indicating that your staff or clients frequently buy a company's products will not boost your chances of success. Corporations have a responsibility to their shareholders and must be able to explain the business reason for their charitable giving program. Providing funding to all the non-profit agencies that use the company's products or services, regardless of the type or quality of their programs, is simply not a good business decision. Ultimately, your proposal will be evaluated on its own merits, not on the shopping patterns of your clients.

Banks frequently have a slightly different perspective regarding non-profits and the use of their corporate services. Most banks expect non-profits that are requesting funding to have an account at their bank. Although having an account will not guarantee funding, failure to have one will most likely result in a denial of your request.

☞ Connecting Through Community Impact

The most effective way to attract a company's interest is by developing a positive presence in the community, and cultivating a reputation as an important and effective community service provider. Focus your energy on **what you do** and what services you provide, not on **who you know**. Although employee involvement will certainly help your funding request, the best way to gain the interest of corporate funders is through the impact your agency has in the community. If you are recognized as an effective service provider and are involved with issues that interest a company, your program is a good candidate for corporate funding. As one manager said,

> **"The funding decision is more about what the non-profit stands for in the community and about the impact it has made. It's not critical to call the CEO and invite her to lunch."**

☞ Introductory Phone Calls

If you are familiar with the funding procedures of most private and family foundations, you probably will make some effort, before submitting your proposal, to contact the funder to introduce your program and ask for suggestions about presenting your project. The process differs slightly for corporate foundations. While it is expected that you will call to request the corporate foundation guidelines, the companies I interviewed were divided on the need or even the desirability of a phone call to discuss your program with a foundation manager, prior to submitting the proposal. (See Figure 4.3.)

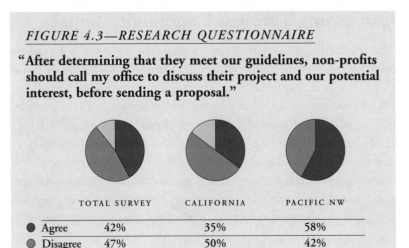

FIGURE 4.3—RESEARCH QUESTIONNAIRE

"After determining that they meet our guidelines, non-profits should call my office to discuss their project and our potential interest, before sending a proposal."

		TOTAL SURVEY	CALIFORNIA	PACIFIC NW
●	Agree	42%	35%	58%
●	Disagree	47%	50%	42%
○	Neither	11%	15%	0%

Here again, there were regional differences in the responses. The positive responses from the Pacific Northwest were in alignment with the greater value companies there seem to place on personal contact and development of relationships as part of the funding decision. At the same time, a lack of clear consensus on the need for a phone call is reflected in the high percentage of disagree responses in all geographic regions. (42% in the Pacific Northwest; 50% in California.) The lack of time most managers have available to answer calls may have contributed to the high negative responses.

Those company representatives who expressed a desire to talk with non-profit agencies before a proposal is submitted, consider the phone call to be a screening process that benefits both the company and the non-profit. The call saves the non-profit from wasting time writing a proposal that does not match the company's funding areas, while also saving the company manager from reading a proposal that does not match the company's funding areas. Others view the calls as a way to assist non-profits by providing them with information about the company's funding procedures, even if the information they provide is a recommendation that the non-profit should apply elsewhere.

Managers who were opposed to receiving phone calls felt it was too difficult to effectively advise a non-profit about a particular program, and its fit with the company's funding interests, without first reviewing a written summary of that program.

If you plan to approach a company for funding and are uncertain about the need to make a call to the foundation manager to introduce your program, identify the procedure preferred by the company before you do anything. When calling for the company's guidelines, ask if it would be acceptable to call again, after you have reviewed the guidelines, to discuss your project before submitting a proposal. If phone calls are accepted, you will be encouraged to call again. Some companies will refer you to hotlines or secretarial staff for answers to basic questions.

If the company encourages phone calls before proposals are sent, make the call. It will be a good opportunity to create a positive first impression and possibly attract the interest of the foundation manager. Use the call to introduce your agency and its work, describe the project and ask if the project seems to be something they might consider funding. A brief call can prevent you from writing a proposal that has no chance of funding.

Most managers, regardless of their opinion about the need for introductory phone calls, indicated that small staff sizes or the demands of their jobs have reduced the amount of time available to effectively respond to calls from non-profits. Therefore, if you decide to call a company to discuss your program, it is important to demonstrate a value for the manager's time by being sufficiently prepared for the call. Chapter 5 includes tips for speaking on the phone with corporate funders.

☞ Increasing Funding Potential Through Coalitions and Partnerships

Many companies expressed a belief that the recent cuts in government funding presage difficult times ahead for non-profit agencies. Most feel that government funding reductions will be permanent and, unlike previous budgetary crises, will not be restored with the next election. Government funding is expected to become more difficult to obtain and according to many managers I interviewed, the key to non-profit survival in the future will be in partnerships and coalitions that unite individual non-profit agencies working on related issues.

Coalitions and partnerships of many non-profit agencies are attractive to funders because they allow leveraging of funds. Coalitions give funders a bigger impact for their dollars since coalitions can offer a more comprehensive solution to the issue, unlike individual non-profits which usually address only one aspect of an issue. Coalitions allow non-profit agencies to combine some administrative functions and reduce the relative overhead expenses while still remaining, to some degree, independent entities. The company representatives cited United Way as an effective coalition. The following are additional examples of non-profit coalitions:

- Five separate non-profit housing agencies, with clients representing five different minority groups, develop a joint project designed to meet the housing needs of all ethnic groups in a community.

- A daycare agency, a senior care agency, a job training agency, an agency offering ESL classes, a health clinic and a food bank create one community social services center that meets the varied needs of the disadvantaged population in their community.

Coalitions of non-profit agencies can be attractive for companies looking to fund creative and innovative solutions to issues. Proposals from a coalition of non-profits also save companies the time needed to review proposals from individual non-profit agencies. Many companies expect to see a trend in the future toward partnerships and coalitions, especially in the metropolitan areas where multiple non-profit agencies serving similar clientele exist, and because of their close geographic proximity, could more easily work together in a coalition.

> **Successful coalitions project an image of non-profit agencies that are farsighted, capable of managing complex operations, financially savvy and team players—all of which are attributes valued by corporations.**

Coalitions represent a novel approach to very old problems and a well-planned coalition can be an attractive candidate for corporate funding. As one manager said,

"The more a non-profit agency can demonstrate that it is working with other non-profits, the more it appears as if it will survive in tomorrow's environment."

However, before you decide to pursue formation of a coalition with other agencies, you should be aware of some of the concerns voiced about the concept by corporate representatives.

The company representatives' biggest concern about coalitions dealt with distribution and tracking of funding. Some companies questioned the ability of a coalition to use funding effectively for the good of the whole, while still maintaining the ability to track the impact of individual grants from separate funders. In other words, how can a company ensure that grant money given to a specific agency is used effectively by the entire coalition? Other companies expressed a concern that combining funds in a coalition lessens the funder's ability to support and develop a relationship with one specific member of the coalition. However, if allowed to direct the way in which their dollars will be spent, more companies expressed a willingness to entertain the possibility of funding a coalition.

Another concern cited about coalitions was the inherent difficulty that arises when attempting to join two or more separate organizations into one. As mergers and acquisitions become more familiar in the business environment, many corporate managers are becoming aware of the problems associated with creating new organizations. Although a coalition does not necessarily involve the complete merger of two separate organizations, corporate managers are still cautious about the ability of non-profits to work together to form an effective partnership. The companies mentioned some very basic issues that frequently stall plans to form a coalition, such as:

- What overhead functions will be combined, and how?

- Will one agency move to the other's location and, if so, which agency will move?

There are also concerns about the challenges facing employees in a newly formed partnership. Issues such as motivation, loyalty and the culture of the agency must be addressed before a partnership is attempted. However, with careful planning, it was felt that many non-profits could benefit from the establishment of a partnership with similar agencies.

> **Forming a coalition of non-profit agencies solely for the sake of attracting corporate funding will doom the idea from its inception.**

The purpose of a coalition is to maximize individual non-profit programs by reducing the cost and increasing the effectiveness, impact and scope of the total range of programs offered to the community. Agencies considering a coalition should think carefully before attempting the process. All the involved agencies need to approach the coalition as equal partners, with similar motivations, desire and capability. As one manager said, "A coalition takes more than three good ideas and four meetings." Member agencies should add value to the services of the other member agencies and not join the coalition simply to be part of something new.

☞ Implications and Recommendations

- Do not turn away from corporate funding because you have no connection within the company. Many companies develop relationships with non-profits only after they have been funded.

- Cultivate employees as a gateway into a company. Create relationships with employees, particularly management employees. Review your membership and client list to determine if any employees are already involved with your agency.

- If your agency does have friends in a company, be cautious in requesting their support. Never ask someone to apply pressure to the corporate funder. Such attempts frequently backfire and can result in rejection of the funding request.

- Personal friendships with corporate employees can provide visibility for your program, but cannot compensate for a poor proposal. Even personal friendships with company executives are of little help to non-profits that do not meet the guidelines. Ultimately, proposals rise and fall on their own merits—how well you fit the guidelines and how well you articulate your impact.

- Increase your visibility in the community. Encourage media coverage of your events; speak out at public events dealing with your area of expertise. Your positive reputation in the community can become your connection to a corporate funder.

- If you are a small, relatively unknown agency, consider delaying the submission of a proposal to a corporate foundation until your agency has more visibility and a record of accomplishments in the community. Instead, consider matching gift programs or requesting support from local company branches.

- Consider aligning with other agencies as a coalition if it will increase the value of services provided to the community. Never form a coalition just to obtain funding. If a coalition seems appropriate, first try working together with the other agencies on a small pilot project. The results will help you evaluate the potential effectiveness of any long-term coalition, and may also help you to identify and avoid possible breakdowns in the partnership.

CHAPTER 5

Characteristics of a Winning Proposal

While it is impossible to predict the outcome of a request for corporate funding, it is possible to identify those factors that tend to reflect positively on a proposal and those factors that tend to reflect negatively. By eliminating as many of the negative factors as possible, and including as many of the positive factors as possible, you can significantly increase your proposal's potential for success.

The next chapters will provide specific suggestions to help you develop a successful proposal. I will discuss the content and format preferred by most of the corporate representatives. I will also identify the attributes of a successful proposal, as well as the most common reasons for rejecting a proposal.

☞ Researching the Company

When asked the most important aspect of writing a proposal, all those interviewed cited the importance of what they termed "doing your homework." This phrase was frequently mentioned during my interviews and refers to the need for non-profit agencies to thoroughly research a company to determine its "fit" with your program.

It is important to find out as much as you can about a company, particularly its areas of funding interest and its proposal requirements, before even beginning to write the document. You want to be certain, before you submit a proposal, that there is a link between the types of services provided by your agency and the company's funding interests. Regardless of how well your proposal is written, if the program needing support does not match the funding interests of the company, you will not receive a grant.

Many company representatives felt that non-profit agencies spend too little time researching companies and, as a result, waste much of their time submitting proposals to companies that are not interested in funding their type of programs.

Many non-profits avoid the research portion of the proposal process because of a mistaken belief that researching a company is too difficult or too time consuming. They instead prefer to use a "shot gun approach"—sending a general proposal to a number of companies, hoping someone will fund them. Not only is this process extremely depressing (you will get very tired of all those rejection letters), it is a huge waste of time and energy.

You may think a company is an ideal candidate for your funding request because it is so successful, or because you and your clients use the company's products. A company may have billions of dollars in revenue, it may make a product used by your children, it may be your favorite place to shop, it may even be located on the same street as your agency, but if that company does not fund programs of the type offered by your agency, you have very little chance of getting funding. Do not waste your time writing a proposal to a company until you are certain it funds your type of program.

A word of caution here. Although it's possible to creatively stretch your program's goals and convince yourself that your program matches the guidelines of almost any company, avoid doing so. Unless your program is a real match, do not send a proposal in the hope that the company will fund you. It won't! Save your time and move on to a more appropriate funding candidate.

You also want to be certain the company funds programs in your geographic area. Many companies have geographic limitations to their funding and will not support programs outside this locality, no matter how closely the program matches the company's areas of interest. Not all companies have geographic limitations to their funding, but generally, the further away a company is located from your agency, the less likely it will be to fund your program, unless your program is regional or national in scope.

"Doing your homework" is not as difficult as you may think. Researching a company is certainly less time consuming than preparing proposals for numerous companies that have absolutely no interest in funding agencies like yours. Start by researching companies headquartered in the community served by your agency, or companies with local branches or offices in that community. You can also research the companies that employ your volunteers and your clients. You can even research companies located in nearby cities.

Your library will most likely have directories to help you identify local companies, as well as companies interested in funding your types of programs. I have found the following directories to be very effective in researching corporations. These directories identify the locations of the headquarters and the subsidiaries of major companies. They also provide general information about each company's area of business, its funding interests and its grant application process. (See Appendix 3 for additional resources for researching corporations.)

National Directory of Corporate Giving, published by The Foundation Center, New York, L. Victoria Hall, Editor. (1-800-424-9836)

National Directory of Corporate Public Affairs, published by Columbia Books, Inc., Washington, D.C., J. Valerie Steele, Editor. (202-898-0662)

You can also uncover information about companies and their executives by scanning business magazines, reading the business section of your local newspaper and surfing company web sites. (Appendix 5 provides Internet locations for a number of corporate web sites.) Many of these corporate web sites include information about the companies' charitable giving programs and their proposal guidelines.

Learn as much as possible about the company and its areas of interest before writing a proposal. You may uncover a number of linkages between the company and your agency that will make your proposal more attractive to the corporate funder.

☞ Techniques for Requesting Guidelines

After you have researched and identified companies that you believe may have some interest or connection with your agency, call the company foundation or their charitable giving office (usually located in the community affairs department), and request the company's guidelines and annual report. If you do not know the foundation's number, call the company's main number and ask to be transferred. If the corporate foundation does not have a copy of the annual report, you many need to call the corporate headquarters.

The company's annual report will give you information about the type of business the company is in, the issues of importance to the company, as well as detailed financial information. You may discover an item in the annual report that you can connect to your agency's work. For example, in the annual report a company may announce plans to open new branches in your community. If the company already has an interest in funding your type of program, they might be willing to support your agency because of its location.

The corporate foundation guidelines will explain the procedure for submitting a proposal to the company. Read the guidelines carefully and remember to check for deadlines. Unlike corporate foundations, some direct corporate giving programs do not publish guidelines; instead, you will probably be instructed to submit a brief letter stating your request.

Even if you believe that you are well-informed about a company's funding procedures and you have the company's guidelines from previous years, call for their current guidelines anyway. There may have been some recent changes to their procedures. Do not rely solely on the grant information printed in corporate directories. That information may also have changed since the directories were published. Supplement the information in the directories with a copy of the current guidelines.

More and more companies are using voice mail systems to handle requests for guidelines and annual reports. Others have a staff member answering these calls. When you call requesting guidelines, this staff member may try to screen your call by asking for information about your program. Do not let this questioning make you nervous. The staff member is only trying to determine if your program is so far beyond the scope of their funding that sending the guidelines won't be of any help to your agency. When you make your call to request guidelines, it's a good idea to be prepared with a few sentences describing your program in the event your call does reach a "live person" instead of voice mail.

Although it may be a little disconcerting to call for guidelines and have a staff member question you about your program, it can actually be a benefit. It's a great opportunity to question the staff person in return. However, if you are able to reach a staff person, do not immediately start down your list of questions. Instead, ask if you can call back with questions after you have reviewed the guidelines. This will demonstrate your value for the staff person's time and will be appreciated. You may find that some of your questions are already answered in the guidelines. The following are examples of questions that can be asked of foundation staff members:

- We believe our ecology program matches your company's interest in funding high school science programs. From my brief description, does our program sound as if it would be of interest to your company? (Remember a positive response only means that your description of the program seems to meet their guidelines, but it does not guarantee funding. Do not get your hopes up too high, yet.)

- We plan to request a grant of $4,500 for our health care program. Does that figure seem reasonable to you?

- Your guidelines indicate deadlines of July 1 and December 1. Would we have a better chance for funding if we applied for the July deadline?

- To whom should the proposal be addressed?

- Does your company also have a matching gift program?

- Your guidelines indicate that you **prefer** to fund agencies located in the Seattle/Tacoma area? Are you also willing to consider proposals from other locations in the state?

Do not argue with the staff person if you are told your agency or program does not fit the corporation's guidelines. After all, the staff person knows the company's guidelines better than you. You can quickly describe another program if you think that it might be more of a fit, but do not hang on the phone describing program after program, searching for something that is a match. Thank the staff person for his time and end the call. Do not think of the call as a rejection, think of it as saving you from submitting a proposal to a company that is not interested in your program.

☞ Telephone Tips

When calling a corporate manager for information or advice, it is important to be prepared for the call. Use the call as an opportunity to create a positive first impression by demonstrating your professionalism.

• Do your homework before calling. Research the company and identify the match between your agency and the company's funding interests.

• Have a specific question or reason for the call. Never call just to tell the foundation manager that you are sending a proposal.

• When you discuss your project on the phone, realize that a positive response from the manager isn't a guarantee of funding. It simply means that your project meets the company's guidelines and will be considered along with all the other eligible applicants.

• You can use the call to assess the company's interest in a particular program. If the manager is not interested in your program, be prepared to describe an alternative. However, do not go through a list of 10 projects hoping you'll eventually interest them in something. This is not a fishing expedition. You are calling to determine the company's level of interest. If there is no interest in the few programs you describe, you'll need to do more research and rethink the value of continuing to pursue support from this particular company.

• If your calls to a company are not returned immediately, be patient. Failure to return calls is not always a sign of rudeness, but frequently is an indication of the manager's lack of time. Wait a week and if you still haven't heard from the company, call again.

Fifteen Ways to Improve the Format and Layout of Your Proposal

The proposal document introduces your agency to a corporation and, unless you have had phone discussions or previous interactions, it is generally the first formal contact between your agency and the corporation. First impressions quite often form a lasting image in the mind of the funder and so it is critical that all components of your proposal package—the document itself, the attachments, even the envelope—present your agency as a professional and business-like organization. The following recommendations to improve your proposal were suggested by the corporate representatives participating in the interviews.

1. Your proposal package must look professional. It should be neatly done and have no spelling or grammatical errors.

From the moment your proposal package arrives on the funder's desk, it is being evaluated. Much of the initial evaluation is informal and may not even be done consciously. Think about the mail you receive at home or in your office. Like most people, you probably develop opinions about the sender before you even open the letter.

What do you think about mail you receive in a soiled, reused envelope, or mail with your name misspelled and your address scrawled illegibly across the front? Corporate funders feel the same as you. A package that appears messy and hastily assembled will convey an image of an incompetent, disorganized agency. Corporations are not interested in attaching their name and their funding to what may be an inept organization.

Although most of the company representatives considered minor grammatical and spelling mistakes to be unavoidable human errors, they also felt that too many mistakes in a proposal might be an indication of an organization that does not focus sufficiently on important details. Submitting a proposal full of errors will likely cause the corporate representatives to wonder if this sloppiness has also impacted the accuracy of other critical documents, such as the agency's budgets and records of donations. While your proposal will not be rejected because of one spelling mistake, numerous errors will certainly have a negative impact on your chances of receiving funding.

So, check and recheck the spelling and grammar in your proposal. If a passage "sounds funny," but you are unsure if there is an actual error, have someone else read it. Do not just submit the proposal hoping the error won't be noticed. Even if you rely on computer software to edit the spelling of your document, it is still a good idea to have someone else read the final draft. Computer software will not identify all errors, such as a correctly spelled but misplaced word.

Most companies understand that non-profits have little time to devote to writing proposals, but they still expect a complete, professional-looking package. If your non-profit agency is to be taken seriously, you need to find the time to write a good proposal. If you do not have sufficient time, wait until you do. Never submit an incomplete or sloppy package hoping the company will take pity on you and fund your request anyway. Remember the company views you as a potential investment. Would you invest your paycheck in a company that appears disorganized and unprofessional?

2. Address the envelope carefully. Check for the correct corporate name and address.

Companies spend an incredible amount of time and money developing a corporate name and a logo, and then creating a sense of loyalty toward that name among their customers and employees. The company's name and logo is a critical component of its culture. It is the company's identity; it is who they are; it differentiates them from their competition.

Most managers felt that non-profit agencies hoping to be seriously considered for funding by a company should at least take the time to identify the correct spelling of the company's name. They felt that a failure to correctly identify the company was an indication of a non-profit's indifference and lack of real interest in developing a partnership with that company. Incorrectly spelling a company's name can also be considered another indication of a lack of focus on details that, as mentioned previously, could cause the company to question the agency's overall ability to keep accurate records. A few company representatives commented that incorrectly identifying the company could result in a rejection of the entire proposal!

The correct use of a corporate name involves more than just the correct spelling. Check capitalization and punctuation, too. Also, be certain that you indicate the complete company name. The need to correctly spell the company name may seem obvious, but it can be confusing. For example:

- "The ABC Company" *is not the same as* "The Abc Company"

- "ABC Company, Inc." *is not the same as* "ABC Company"

- "The ABC Computer Graphics Company" *is not the same as* "The ABC Computer Company"

- "A.B.C. Company" *is not the same as* "ABC Company"

Many companies separate their corporate giving program from their corporate foundation. Are you certain you addressed your proposal to the appropriate program?

- "The ABC Company" *or to* "The ABC Company Foundation"

Do not confuse the company's product with the company's name. Be certain you are sending your proposal to the company and not to the product. For example, there is no SEGA Genesis Company and no Apple Macintosh Computer Company. If you are uncertain about the correct way to address your proposal, call the company for input before mailing your material.

3. *Do not send anything that resembles a form letter. If possible, address the proposal to a person and not just to the company.*

If the company accepts phone calls, contact them and determine to whom the proposal should be addressed. Even if the company's guidelines lists names, call and recheck those names. Employees frequently change jobs and guidelines are not necessarily rewritten every year. The names in the guidelines may no longer be correct. If calls are not accepted, address the proposal to the name indicated in the current copy of the guidelines, but be certain you are looking at **current** guidelines. While no one will criticize a proposal sent to a manager who just recently left his position, your proposal will be viewed negatively if it is sent to a manager who left five years ago. Again, the impression will be that your agency does not focus on details.

When mailing a proposal to a specific person, correct spelling is again critical. We live in a culturally diverse society and "traditional" names and spellings are no longer the norm. Do not assume you know the correct spelling. Ask for the correct spelling of managers' names even if you believe their name is commonly used. Many names are not spelled as they sound. *John Smith* may be spelled *Jon Symthe.* You should also be conscious of the fact that not all names are gender specific. A male manager who constantly receives his mail addressed to *Mrs. Leslie Smith* will be positively impressed when he receives your proposal addressed to *Mr. Leslie Smith.*

If you are unable to determine the correct name, address the document to the company, but avoid general salutations like "Dear Corporate Executive" or "Dear Friend." These may be appropriate for a general direct mail campaign, but most company representatives consider these to be form letters and frequently discard these proposals without reading them.

4. Do not attempt to bypass the corporate foundation staff.

Attempting to gain a company's interest by mailing your letter of inquiry or proposal directly to the CEO instead of the corporate foundation staff is an ineffective tactic. The first person to look through an executive's mail is rarely the executive. Secretaries generally sort the mail. Unless you know the CEO personally or were told to send the document to his office, your proposal will be rerouted by the secretary back to the corporate foundation staff before it is seen by the executive. The time required to move your proposal from the executive's mailbox, through the corporate mail system and back to the corporate foundation staff could cause your proposal to miss the deadline and result in a rejection for that reason.

5. Avoid indiscriminate "mass mailings." Personalize each proposal package.

In this age of computers, it is tempting to write a general proposal and send copies to a number of different companies. I do not suggest this approach unless the companies' guidelines specifically state that they accept proposals written for other funders.

It is acceptable, however, to submit one proposal to a number of companies that have similar guidelines and funding interests, if you find a way to personalize the proposal for each individual company. For example, do not just copy and mail the exact same document to a list of companies. Instead, in the cover letter, include a statement identifying the match between your agency and the funding interests of the particular company. Also, remember to change the company's name and address on the cover letter, and be sure you refer to the correct company throughout the proposal. Most company representatives talked of receiving proposals that included references to another company in the narrative. While this is generally not reason for denial of your proposal, it will not contribute favorably to the overall impression of your agency.

6. Suggest; do not tell.

Do not "tell" a funder that they will be interested in your program. For example, avoid statements such as, "We know ABC Company will be very interested in our project because...." Instead, present your case and let the funder determine their level of interest. Use statements such as, "We believe our program matches the ABC Company's interest in the arts because...." Do not tell funders what they should think about your program. Educate and inform them, and then allow the companies to make their own decision.

7. Utilize a layout that is easy to read.

The appearance of the proposal can have a subtle impact on the reader's frame of mind. A proposal with an appealing layout can help to attract and hold the interest of the reader, while proposals that are exceedingly long, contain many pages of attachments and are typed in tiny font can appear boring and difficult to read.

Since your proposal may be read at the end of a long day after the manager has already read 30 other proposals, the layout of the document may determine the level of interest the manager brings to your proposal. Company representatives offered the following suggestions for improving a proposal's layout:

Effective Proposal Layout

- If the guidelines set a page limit, do not exceed it. Even one paragraph more than the limit is unacceptable.

- Ten point is the minimum font size (12 point is preferred). Margins should be one inch.

- Summarize information into bullets points or simple charts wherever possible.

- Use black ink only, and white or off-white paper. All other colors are a strain on the eyes.

- Avoid "walls of words." Conservative use of bolding, underlining and spacing can ensure that the important points are not lost amid paragraphs and paragraphs of words. However, too much bolding and underlining can make the page appear confusing.

- Information requested in the guidelines should be easy to find and not lost in the narrative. Respond to questions in the same order as they appear in the guidelines, and use the same wording.

- If your agency has a web site, be sure to mention it. It provides a way for interested companies to learn more about your agency without having to read additional pages of a proposal.

8. The narrative should be complete and logical.

The narrative should flow easily and show a clear vision. Your overall plan should seem feasible and your argument should be cogent. There should be no unclear or unexplained points.

Some non-profits erroneously assume that a company will contact them if any part of the proposal is unclear or if requested information is missing. While that is generally true for proposals that have passed the initial review and are being seriously considered for funding, it is not always true for every proposal that lands in the company's offices. The volume of proposals received by companies prohibits additional investigation of any but the most competitive proposals. A lack of clarity or a lack of completeness may keep your proposal from receiving the serious consideration that it deserves.

9. Adopt a writing style that is brief, clear and to the point.

Corporations are accustomed to a style of writing that is brief, clear and to the point. This style of writing may take some practice, but it is the style most familiar to business people and, therefore, it is expected of anyone communicating with a company, even non-profit agencies seeking funding. A proposal that utilizes this business style of writing will be factual, devoid of excessive emotion and will state the basic who, what, where, when and why. It will avoid flowery narrative to describe a program such as, "Happy children playing merrily in the school yard." Scenarios such as this may be entertaining, but are not very effective. Companies are not swayed by excessive emotion, but are more interested in factual statements, such as the number of children served by your program and the program's impact on their lives.

10. Avoid jargon and labels.

The terminology used in the proposal should be easily understood and devoid of any jargon. Do not use abbreviations or acronyms even if you believe they are generally understood. The words may be commonly used in your agency and understood by people associated with your issue, but they may not be understood by the general public or by the managers reviewing your proposal.

When describing your clients, avoid use of nebulous terms, such as "underserved" or "at risk" children. Although these terms may be clear to those working in your agency, they can be interpreted in many different ways by those not as familiar with the field. Instead, use phrases that more specifically describe the population or clientele, such as "children of single-parent families" or "poverty-level income families" or "children with gang involvement or police records."

It's best to have your final draft read by someone who is unfamiliar with your agency in order to determine how effectively the proposal communicates your major points. If a proposal is well written, the reader should not have any questions about the program after reading the document.

11. The information in your proposal must be accurate.

If you include facts or statistics, be certain they are accurate. Do not try to embellish your agency's reputation by stretching the truth, and do not omit requested information because of a concern that it might have a negative impact.

A company may never realize that you intentionally included inaccurate information, but if the error is discovered, your proposal will immediately be denied and future requests for funding may be denied also. More importantly, your agency's reputation will be tarnished and the incident will probably be communicated to other funders, potentially damaging your chances for obtaining support from other corporations.

12. Proposals should look professional, not expensive.

Recognize that your proposal is a marketing tool that will help persuade a company to invest in your agency. The document's professional appearance and content should attract interest. However, avoid slick packages such as glossy binders, or gimmicks like triple folding paper. You may think the unusual packaging will make the proposal more interesting, but it will be difficult to read and will appear as if you are wasting money. Using color is also considered an unnecessary expense since the company will probably make black and white copies of your document for their board members.

13. *Attach only the material that is requested or that is pertinent to your case.*

Always include whatever attachments the company requests. The most commonly requested attachments include: the agency's 501(c)(3) IRS letter, list of board members and their affiliations, financial statements, list of other funders, and the agency and program budgets. A **few** letters of recommendation can be effective, especially if they are written by company employees. Overall, if you are uncertain about the need to attach an item, it's probably best not to include it. Remember that **bigger is not better.** A long proposal with many attachments will be very difficult to read.

If you do not have a particular document that has been requested by a company, it is necessary to explain the reason and not simply ignore the request. Either attach a statement explaining the omission, or call the company to explain. Most company representatives understand the difficulty non-profits have developing proposals and are generally willing to suggest alternatives to the information they need. For example, many grassroots agencies do not have audited financial statements and most companies will, if asked, accept financials that are not audited.

Attaching a few, selected news clippings can also be effective, but do not attach every clipping ever received by your agency. Carefully choose the clippings to be attached. They should be current and, if possible, reflect media recognition given to another one of your funders as a result of their support of your agency. Media attention is one reason companies support non-profit organizations and your ability to attract media coverage of your funders is appealing to potential corporate funders.

Almost all the companies I interviewed agreed that attaching a video explaining your program is unnecessary and could also be viewed as a waste of money. Most of the company representatives said they do not have easy access to a VCR, nor do they have the time to view the tape. If your agency has a video, mention it in your proposal, but do not send it with your proposal. If the company is interested in viewing the tape, they will contact you for a copy.

14. Consider the timing of your submission.

Follow the guidelines or call the company to determine the best time to send a proposal. Do not wait until the last minute to send your document. Mail your document so that it arrives at least a few weeks before the due date. Do not use an expensive overnight delivery service. Companies will wonder why you are willing to "waste" money on expensive mailing when better planning would have allowed you to use less expensive U.S. Mail.

Some corporations allow proposals to be submitted via e-mail. If the company allows electronic transmission of proposals, it's a good idea to call the company after transmitting your proposal to be certain the e-mail was received.

If a company does not have deadlines and accepts grants all year long, submit your proposal during the first or second quarter to ensure adequate funding is available. It's best not to wait until the end of the year. While some companies allocate a certain portion of their total budget to each quarter, others distribute the dollars until the budget for that year is exhausted. So even though your proposal may be of interest to the company, if it is received after the money for that year has already been spent, it will not be funded. If your proposal was not funded because the budget was already spent, some companies will give your proposal priority consideration the following year. However, most companies will instead require you to reapply and take your chances with everyone else the following year.

Recognize that it takes time to reach a funding decision. It can take up to 12 weeks to review a proposal and make a decision. Companies with more complicated review processes, involving multiple stages and committees, may take even longer. Decisions regarding larger grants may only be determined once a year at corporate board meetings. Do not call a company a week after mailing your proposal to check the status. Instead, wait at least four to five weeks before calling for status of your proposal.

15. *Do not become discouraged if your proposal is not approved.*

Although disappointment following a denial of funding is understandable and perhaps even healthy, it is important to recognize that denials are a normal part of the process of seeking funding. A rejection of your proposal does not necessarily mean that your proposal was poorly written and it does not necessarily mean that your agency's program is without worth. If you followed the company's guidelines, it is very possible that the reason for the rejection was an issue completely beyond your control.

Frequently, a change in the company is the reason for denial of your request for funding. There may have been an unexpected downturn in the company's profits that caused a reduction in the corporate foundation's budget, or the company's Board of Directors may have decided to change the funding priorities and focus their philanthropic dollars in another area, or perhaps all the charitable dollars allocated for the year had already been distributed to other non-profits and there simply was no more funding available for your program.

The important thing to remember is not to give up. Do not let a rejection or two cause you to completely turn away from corporate funding. Learn whatever you can from each rejection and move on to the next funder. After all, your next attempt might be successful!

☞ Implications and Recommendations

- Do your homework. Thoroughly research companies before sending a proposal.

- Even if you have a company's guidelines from last year, call for current guidelines and an annual report. There may have been recent changes.

- Follow the guidelines **exactly.** Do not assume that submitting a general proposal will meet the requirements of all companies. A number of company representatives said they do not even read proposals that they felt were written without referring to their guidelines. This is not done to be purposely malicious, but is done because the companies want to be fair to those agencies that did take the time to research the company and follow the guidelines.

- If you decide to send the same proposal to a number of different companies, include a statement in the body of the document explaining the connection between your agency and each different company. Review the document to ensure you have not inadvertently forgotten to delete the names of the other companies.

- Create a professional-looking proposal package, but avoid slick, expensive-looking materials.

- Avoid form letters. Personalize each package. Address each document to a specific person.

- Check the spelling of the name of the company and the foundation manager.

- Use a layout that is easy to read. Avoid "walls of words." Be brief, clear and concise. Avoid jargon. Ask a friend to read the proposal for grammatical errors and for clarity.

- Attach only the material that is requested or that is essential to understanding the proposal.

- Avoid using expensive overnight mail services. Complete your proposal early enough to allow for use of U.S. Mail.

CHAPTER 6
Essential Components of a Proposal

☞ **Letters of Inquiry**

More companies are beginning to request a letter of inquiry before a full proposal is submitted. Similar to introductory phone calls, this is seen as a way to quickly screen out those agencies and programs that do not match the company's interests, and also save the non-profit from taking the time to write a full proposal that does not have a chance of being funded. These short letters provide sufficient information for the company to determine if the program is within their funding parameters. Companies that require a letter of inquiry will indicate this in their guidelines.

I am aware of some non-profit agencies that always send a full proposal to corporations, even if a letter of inquiry is requested. These non-profits may already have written a full proposal and do not want to rewrite it into a shorter format. Others believe that sending their entire proposal package will somehow increase their chances of getting funded, even though the guidelines specifically state that a short letter is required. According to the companies I interviewed, ignoring requests for a short letter of inquiry and submitting a full proposal instead, will be a waste of your time. This tactic will create the perception that your agency is unable to follow directions and may damage your chances of receiving funding.

If a letter of inquiry is requested, it should be concise and should not exceed two to three pages. (The guidelines will sometimes indicate a page limit.) In the letter, explain the mission of your agency, cite key achievements to establish your credibility and indicate the reason the company might be interested in your program. Clearly explain your program and your objectives. Describe what is needed from the company, giving a specific dollar amount. Brevity and the ability to make your case quickly and concisely is critical when writing a letter of inquiry. Some companies make funding decisions based on the letter of inquiry. Others will request a full proposal if the program described in the letter of inquiry is of interest to them.

If a company requires a full proposal, provide all the information requested, in the order it was requested. In most cases, full corporate proposals should not exceed 10 pages of narrative. (Again, check company guidelines for page limitations.) Use the company's wording when responding to specific questions. If a full proposal is required, but no specific outline is provided, your proposal should include the following components:

Components of a Successful Proposal

- Executive Summary

- Background Information: Credentials, Mission and Connection to the Company's Interests

- The Problem or Need

- Program Objectives

- Plans for Achieving the Objectives

- Evaluation Plans to Measure Success

Your proposal should also contain financial information. Most companies will want to review the project and the organizational budgets, as well as a list of other funders. Financial information will be discussed in Chapter 7.

☞ Executive Summary

Beginning the proposal with a one page (maximum) executive summary of the proposal's salient points, including the amount of your request, is an effective way to communicate your case. Some companies prefer the summary at the beginning of the proposal, while others like a summary in the cover letter. Both options help the reader understand the entire context of the request before they read the details of the proposal. Summaries also help refresh the reader's memory and can be particularly helpful when the reader has reviewed a large number of proposals at one sitting. Facts can be easily confused and details forgotten, particularly when a number of proposals address similar programs. A summary helps the reader keep the facts clear and organized. When writing a summary for your proposal or cover letter, be certain it is brief and to the point.

☞ # Background Information: Credentials, Mission and Connection to the Company's Interests

1. Credentials

All companies agreed that the most effective indicator of an agency's credibility are its accomplishments and successes, and so your proposal should always include a **few statements** of accomplishments. The agency's accomplishments provide a track record and history of positive impact in the community, and demonstrate the agency's capability to successfully complete projects. Accomplishments have the greatest impact when described in concrete, statistical terms. For example:

- *Ineffective Accomplishment:* In 1997, we helped many children improve their reading skills.

- *Effective Accomplishment:* 75% of the 125 children in our program in 1997 improved their reading skills by two grade levels.

Interestingly, most of the companies did not consider the awards received by an agency to be a good indicator of that agency's capability. Companies are rarely impressed by a list of awards since the source of the award and the selection criteria is generally unknown by the company, and so the overall importance of the honor is difficult to determine.

Companies are interested, however, in testimonials from clients. Many companies consider testimonials to be an acceptable method of demonstrating an agency's accomplishments. This is particularly important for a new agency without a track record of more concrete accomplishments. Letters from clients describing the agency's positive impact on their lives, can help establish the agency's credibility and capability to successfully complete projects.

2. Mission and Connection to the Company

When stating their mission, non-profits should try to include a statement connecting the agency to the company's interests. This connection need not be complicated and can be established in as little as one sentence. The following is an example:

• Recognizing the ABC Company Foundation's interest in funding health programs for senior citizens, we believe you may be interested in our innovative senior care program. Our mission is to provide high-quality, affordable health care to all senior citizens in Portland, regardless of their ability to pay.

Your ability to link your program with the company's interests demonstrates that you are willing to take the time to **do your homework.** You have not just done random mailings of your proposal, but have instead read the guidelines and identified the match between the company's funding areas and your program.

☞ The Problem or Need

Unlike most private foundations that routinely require non-profit agencies to define the problem they are attempting to solve, companies disagreed about the need to include a problem definition section in proposals seeking their funding. Some companies saw no need for a problem statement. Those that did require a problem statement conceded that it is not an essential portion of a proposal.

Many companies felt that non-profit agencies devote too much space in the proposals to defining the problem and insufficient space to describing their plans to eliminate the problem. Other companies, particularly those serving rural constituencies, felt that the community problems were already well known and so they did not require non-profits to document the problem in the proposal. Others felt that defining the problem was necessary only to substantiate the importance of a less obvious issue in the community.

Should you include a problem statement in your proposal? Definitely, if it is requested in the guidelines. Otherwise, it depends on the type of proposal. If your agency is newly established, statistical data can be an effective way to demonstrate the need for your program. As previously discussed, statistics can identify the scope of the problem and demonstrate that your agency is not merely duplicating current efforts in the community, but is satisfying a need not met by existing agencies.

> **Most companies agreed that new agencies planning to offer services similar to those already existing in a community must include a problem statement in their proposal that justifies the necessity for their programs.**

Statistical problem statements are also effective when the problem or the scope of the problem you are addressing is not widely known or understood. Requests for larger than average grants should also include a problem statement to substantiate the need for the larger sum.

In all cases, keep the problem statement short and include hard facts, not just anecdotal comments. Problem statements that are based entirely on personal knowledge of staff members and include no statistical data at all were considered ineffective. As one manager said, "Too many issues are determined by gut feel."

> **It was felt that personal knowledge must be supported by statistical facts in order to effectively define the problem that an agency is attempting to resolve.**

A few statistics are all that is necessary. In fact, most companies cautioned against including too much data in the proposal. Multiple pages of statistics can make the problem seem overwhelming and cause funders to question if their small grant can really have a measurable impact on the problem.

The focal point of your proposal should be your **solution,** not the problem. If attachments are permitted, consider including a recent study, news clipping or fact sheet explaining the problem in detail. Then, instead of writing a paragraph or two on the problem, you can just reference the attachment. This saves the reader from spending time reviewing material that may already be familiar to them, but still demonstrates your agency's connection to the community and awareness of the extent of the local problem.

Unless your agency focuses on national issues, the statistics cited in your proposal must pertain to the **local or regional** problem. Including figures describing the problem on a national scale will do little to support the need for your community program. Sources for statistics vary according to the scope of the subject you are researching. The following are a few sources for local statistics:

- Local library

- United Way

- Police Department

- Chamber of Commerce

- City Department of Social Services.

Government data also can be helpful when defining a regional or national problem, and is available on the Internet. The following are useful sites:

- *Census Bureau:* http://www.census.gov

- *The Bureau of Labor Statistics:* http://stats.bls.gov/blshome.html

- *Federal Data:* http://www.fedstats.gov

- *Federal Budget:* http://www.access.gpo.gov/su_docs/budget98/maindown.html

- *U.S. Environmental Protection Agency:* http://www.epa.gov

- *Department of Education:* http://gcs.ed.gov

☞ Program Objectives

Corporate employees are very familiar with objectives. For most corporate employees, their work performance is evaluated and their salary is determined by their ability to meet objectives. The value of most corporate projects is determined by the objectives that were achieved. The development and achievement of objectives is a major aspect of corporate business, and so it is understandable that the program objectives are an essential element of a proposal to corporate funders.

> **The ability of a non-profit agency to express its program in terms of concrete, measurable objectives has increased in importance as demand for corporate funding increases.**

Companies can no longer afford to support programs that seem "nice" or sound "interesting." Companies determine the value of an agency or a project by its objectives. Objectives are considered so crucial to understanding an agency's funding request, that many companies now consider the outcomes or objectives to be one of most important parts of the proposal.

Company representatives felt that objectives frequently are too loosely defined. They caution agencies to avoid vague objectives that state nothing more than "We plan to do good work and solve the problem," and instead, focus on creating outcome-based objectives.

Objectives can also be quantitative or qualitative, and sometimes, a combination of both. Quantitative objectives express the expected change or impact in terms of a **specific, measurable quantity.** For example:

• "Our objective is to reduce the number of homeless families in this community by 25% in 24 months through the construction of 125 low-income housing units."

This quantitative objective expresses the expected outcome of the program through use of a specific, measurable quantity—a 25% reduction in the number of homeless families.

Qualitative objectives express the expected change or impact in terms of **a quality, an attribute, or some characteristic or trait.** For example:

- "The objective for the next 18 months of our youth symphony program is to increase elementary school children's understanding and appreciation of classical music through exposure to five youth symphonies."

This qualitative objective expresses the expected outcome of the program through the use of a quality—increased music appreciation and understanding.

Company representatives generally considered quantitative objectives to be more effective than qualitative objectives. This is not surprising since companies are accustomed to setting their own objectives using measurable, quantitative data. (See Figure 6.1.)

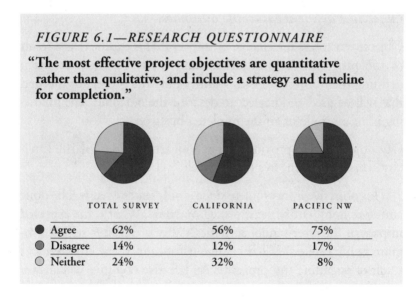

FIGURE 6.1—RESEARCH QUESTIONNAIRE

"The most effective project objectives are quantitative rather than qualitative, and include a strategy and timeline for completion."

	TOTAL SURVEY	CALIFORNIA	PACIFIC NW
● Agree	62%	56%	75%
◐ Disagree	14%	12%	17%
○ Neither	24%	32%	8%

The following are general characteristics of effective objectives that are applicable to both quantitative and qualitative objectives:

> **Characteristics of Program Objectives**
>
> 1. Objectives define measurable outcomes.
>
> 2. Objectives express how you will achieve the outcome.
>
> 3. Objectives include a timeline for achieving the outcome.
>
> 4. Objectives are realistic and achievable.
>
> 5. Objectives are not too broad.
>
> 6. Objectives are in alignment with the agency's mission.

1. Objectives define measurable outcomes.

Objectives express the change or impact that is expected as a result of the program. A common mistake made by agencies when defining their objectives is to identify only the process or method that will be used and neglect to describe the outcome. The following is an example of an incomplete objective:

• "Our objective is to provide after-school art activities for 100 inner city school children, five days a week."

This objective is incomplete since it only states what will be done and does not identify the expected outcome. What is the expected impact of the after-school activities? Why is the after-school program being offered? What change will occur in the children as a result of attending this program? An effective objective will answer these questions. This same objective can be improved by including the expected outcome of the after-school program. For example:

• "Our objective is to reduce gang-related crime in the community by 15% in 12 months by providing after-school art activities for 100 inner city school children, five days a week."

With the addition of the expected outcome, the objective clearly indicates the measurable impact that is expected in the community as a result of the program. Without the inclusion of the outcome, it may seem that the agency is uncertain about the reason for offering their program.

2. Objectives express how you will achieve the outcome.

Objectives include a statement of the strategy to achieve the outcome. For example:

- "Our objective is to reduce the number of homeless families in this community by 25% in 24 months *with the construction of 125 low-income housing units.*"

  OR

- "The objective of our youth symphony program, for the next 18 months, is to increase elementary school children's understanding and appreciation of classical music *through exposure to five youth symphonies.*"

3. Objectives include a timeline for achieving the outcome.

You must include a statement that defines the amount of time you believe is required to achieve the objective. For example:

- "Our objective is to reduce the number of homeless families in this community by 25% *in 24 months* with the construction of 125 additional low-income housing units."

  OR

- "The objective of our youth symphony program, *for the next 18 months,* is to increase elementary school children's understanding and appreciation of classical music through exposure to five youth symphonies.

4. Objectives are realistic and achievable.

To claim your program will increase reading levels by five grade levels in 12 months sounds too good to be true. Unless you can prove having achieved this level of success in the past, it's better to plan for more modest outcomes. Objectives that seem unrealistically positive may be interpreted by corporations as a sign that your program is not well thought out, and they may assume that your agency has an inaccurate view of the true scope of the problem. Concerns about an agency's understanding of the issue can negatively impact that agency's chances of being funded.

It is also important to be realistic about the number of objectives included in a proposal. One to three objectives is sufficient for the average-sized corporate grant. More is not better. Including ten objectives will not impress a corporate funder; instead, it can indicate that the agency has an unrealistic view of the issue and lacks clarity in planning the program.

5. Objectives are not too broad.

No organization can expect to achieve an objective such as "eliminating crime" or "finding jobs for all unemployed people." These are both admirable missions that can guide the overall direction of your agency, but they are unrealistic objectives.

Mission statements are broad in scope, but objectives are more narrow and specific. You may be working toward eliminating crime in the neighborhood **someday,** but your objective for the next 12 months is, most likely, a percentage reduction in crime. If your objectives are too broad, your entire proposal becomes questionable.

It is important to recognize that objectives do not always need to indicate plans for growth. It's appropriate to recognize when your agency has reached its capacity and instead of seeking additional clients and offering new programs, you plan to strengthen and develop the capability of your staff and board. Your objectives, in this case, will relate more to developing a particular skill in your staff.

6. Objectives are in alignment with the agency's mission.

Program objectives should be related to the overall mission of your agency. Some non-profits attempt to develop new programs that are in strong alignment with the funding interests of a particular company, but only loosely related to their own core mission, in order to become eligible for a grant from that company. Corporations tend to avoid funding agencies of this type; agencies that appear to be "chasing the money" and creating new programs simply to meet a company's funding guidelines. If none of your programs match a company's funding interests, do not try to create new programs just to become eligible for funding. Simply move on and research another company as a funding source.

☞ Plans for Achieving the Objectives

After defining the objectives, the proposal should explain the strategies for achieving these objectives. This is the main section of the proposal where you explain your plans, actions and the projected timeline required to achieve your objectives. This is the section that showcases your agency and the value your agency adds to the community. This is your opportunity to market your agency as a worthwhile investment for the company.

Explain your plans in a way that demonstrates innovation, involvement with the community and a unique approach to solving the problem. While companies will fund programs that duplicate proven, successful plans already put in place by other agencies, they prefer to fund unique, innovative programs that propose new approaches to old problems. Innovation does not imply that your program should be controversial, nor does it mean your program should be risky. It does mean that your agency has carefully thought out and thoroughly planned a new way of meeting an ongoing community need. Remember to be clear and concise. Limit emotional narrative and stick with the facts.

☞ Evaluation Plans to Measure Success

Including a section explaining your plans to evaluate the success of your program can increase the value of the proposal. Most companies feel that funding requests should always include an evaluation plan, although they admitted that the evaluation tends to be the weakest section of the proposals they receive. (See Figure 6.2.)

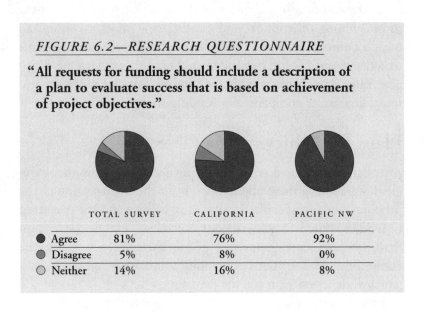

FIGURE 6.2—RESEARCH QUESTIONNAIRE

"All requests for funding should include a description of a plan to evaluate success that is based on achievement of project objectives."

	TOTAL SURVEY	CALIFORNIA	PACIFIC NW
● Agree	81%	76%	92%
● Disagree	5%	8%	0%
○ Neither	14%	16%	8%

Corporations understand that non-profits have limited time and money to spend on formal evaluations, and so most do not require an expensive, time-consuming evaluation process. However, companies believe that evaluations are important to understanding the success of the programs they have funded and they look more favorably on proposals that have included some process to evaluate the program's success. As funding becomes more competitive, more corporations will begin to require non-profits to evaluate and report on the outcomes of the programs supported by their funds.

1. The importance of program evaluation to the corporation.

Corporations use program evaluations to determine the effectiveness of their charitable giving program. If the charitable programs supported by a company have no measurable impact in the community, there may be little reason for a company to continue its grant-making program, while extremely positive results may motivate a company to increase its grantmaking.

In addition, stockholders closely analyze any use of company funds that does not contribute to profits. Without demonstrated community impact, stockholders may question the need for a company's philanthropic programs and may demand that charitable giving be reduced or eliminated completely. As a result, more corporate foundation boards are beginning to inquire about the impact of their company's grantmaking.

Including an evaluation component in your proposal, and later informing the company of the evaluation results, will help the foundation staff make a compelling case for continuing the company's grantmaking program, and will make your agency a more attractive ongoing investment.

2. The importance of program evaluation to the non-profit agency.

As more non-profit agencies request corporate funding, the entire funding process is becoming more competitive. Program evaluation can help a non-profit agency differentiate itself from the other agencies competing for the same corporate dollar. For example, a non-profit can use an evaluation component to demonstrate that its program serves more clients, at a lower cost, than similar agencies in the community. The evaluation allows the non-profit agency to describe its program as the most cost-effective service of its type in the community and, therefore, a better investment for the company.

Evaluations also help non-profits receive subsequent grants from companies. Program evaluation demonstrates that a non-profit agency is truly interested in providing the best service possible, and is willing to spend the necessary time to evaluate results and identify areas where their program can be improved. This attribute is very attractive to corporations since it indicates a level of maturity and accountability not always found in non-profit agencies. Companies are becoming less interested in funding agencies that just take the grant money and then sever all ties to the company. In fact, most companies said they would rarely provide a second grant to a non-profit if that agency failed to provide some type of evaluative report describing the results of the first grant.

3. The importance of program evaluation to others in the field.

Program evaluation is also a learning tool that can help improve similar programs offered by other agencies. By implementing the successful aspects of your program, similar agencies can increase the effectiveness of the total range of services offered to a community.

> **By evaluating the impact of their program and identifying the aspects that were successful and those that were unsuccessful, a non-profit agency makes a significant contribution to the entire field.**

Without some type of evaluation of results, even a good program may stagnate and cease to improve, depriving clients of the program's full potential and preventing the optimal use of the grantmakers funds.

4. Characteristics of program evaluation.

The evaluations required by large foundations that give away millions of dollars can be formal, expensive, and time-consuming and may even require the services of an outside evaluator unaffiliated with the agency. Nothing so elaborate is needed for the average-sized corporate grant. Most corporations simply want to know your plans for identifying the impact of the company's funding.

An evaluation plan explains the process that will be used to identify the overall effectiveness of your program. It explains the strategies you will use to determine if the program objectives were achieved. A good evaluation plan answers the questions:

- How will you know if you were able to achieve the objectives you set for the program?

- How will you determine if your program is successful?

For capital campaigns or programs that are adding to existing capacity, the plan for evaluation is simple. For example, you simply report whether or not the building was built; whether or not the homeless shelter added the expected number of beds. Including statements that evaluate the cost-effectiveness of the project, such as the total cost vs. expected cost, adds to the effectiveness of an evaluation of a capital campaign.

Evaluation of service programs should include descriptive information also, including the number of people served, demographics of the clients, and actual cost as opposed to expected cost. Most importantly, the evaluation of service programs must determine the overall impact to the clients.

For example, when evaluating a program to tutor children, merely reporting the number of students involved in the program is insufficient. Similar to objectives, your evaluation plan must measure the impact on the participants. An evaluation plan can be creative and it can be unorthodox, but it must include a method to measure impact. The following is an effective plan to evaluate a tutoring program:

• We will evaluate our tutoring program by comparing program participants with students in the same school and grade who did not participate in the program. We will measure and compare variables, such as changes in grade point average, retention levels, attendance levels and acceptance into college.

An evaluation should demonstrate that the non-profit has identified the most appropriate measures of program success. For example, when evaluating the results of a midnight basketball program designed to reduce gang involvement, the evaluation should not report the number of games won or lost, since that is not a measure of program success. The evaluation should refer, instead, to reduction in gang involvement.

A common misconception is that some programs cannot be evaluated because they involve behavioral changes in participants. Yet, if you cannot evaluate the impact of your program, how can you determine if the program is successful? Behavioral changes may be more difficult to evaluate than a program to build a new hospital wing, for example, but with some creative thinking, an effective evaluation plan can be developed.

When evaluating programs that involve behavioral changes, the use of questionnaires or surveys can be helpful. A comparison of participants' responses before and after the program can measure changes in behavior and attitude resulting from the program. Surveys can also be administered to individuals who come in contact with the program's participants, such as teachers and parents. These evaluations are not as strong as those that utilize numeric data, but they do provide credible information on the success of the program. For example:

- We will evaluate our ability to increase leadership skills in students by comparing anecdotal comments from a questionnaire completed, at the beginning and end of the program, by the participants and their teachers. The questionnaire will measure attitude, leadership and behavioral changes noted in the participants.

> **The best evaluation for your agency is one that accurately measures the success of your program by comparing the objectives you planned to achieve with the program's actual outcomes.**

5. Reporting your program evaluation.

Grants above $10,000 usually require some type of formal results feedback. Many companies will provide specific questions and a due date for response. Capital campaigns and grants of $25,000 or more may require periodic progress reports throughout the term of the project. For the average-sized corporate grant of $5,000 or less, there may be a less formalized process. The companies may merely expect a report of the evaluation results to be included when submitting a proposal the following year.

Most corporations will explain their expectations for reporting results when they mail the grant check. If no reporting process is defined, be sure to contact the company to determine their preferred method of reporting program results. Do not assume that the company is not interested in your results because they did not specify a procedure for reporting results. Lack of time sometimes prevents companies from requesting evaluation reports, but most are interested in the results of their funding.

It is critical that non-profit agencies remember to submit any required progress reports by the due dates. Immediately upon receiving a grant, note any due dates on a calendar and assign completion of the progress report to a specific staff member. If the funded project is not completed by the due date, send a report with whatever partial results you have, or call the company and ask for an extension. Do not simply ignore a due date without some kind of communication to the company. Failure to do so may not only disqualify you from future funding from this company, but your agency's poor reputation may be communicated to other corporate funders. Even if a company does not formally request evaluation results, non-profit agencies should take a proactive stand and submit a short report of results.

Be honest in reporting your program's results. Explain what actually happened, and do not attempt to embellish results that seem inadequate. If your program did not achieve the anticipated results, you must still send a report. Explain the reasons for the unexpected results, and any changes or upgrades planned for the program as a result of the shortfall. Companies have quite a bit of experience with their own internal programs that fail to meet expected outcomes. Failure to achieve results will not disqualify your agency for subsequent funding, particularly if you can demonstrate the knowledge your agency gained from the failure.

Similar to writing a proposal, the evaluation results should be written in a clear and concise manner. Copies of media coverage of the program's results can be included, especially if the company's name is mentioned as a supporter.

☞ Implications and Recommendations

- Always contact a company to determine if they require a letter of inquiry or a full proposal. When writing the proposal, follow their guidelines, do not exceed the maximum number of pages and answer questions in the order given.

- It is impossible to identify all the reasons that might cause a proposal to be rejected, but by following the guidelines exactly, you will eliminate as many negatives as possible.

- Develop a one-page summary describing the major points of your program. This can serve as a concise "script" to guide phone conversations with the funder.

- Use statistics prudently. Too many can be boring and will lose the reader, but a **few, local** statistics can make your case stronger.

- A short problem or need statement can effectively set the context for your program, but devote most of the proposal to your plans to solve the problem.

- Express your program in terms of concrete, measurable objectives that clearly define the expected outcomes. Be certain your objectives are realistic and achievable.

- The agency's mission can be broad in scope, but program objectives are specific and few in number.

- New agencies need to differentiate themselves from established agencies by offering a new approach to an existing problem.

- Corporations recognize the value of program evaluations, but usually receive proposals without evaluation plans. Include in your proposal a simple plan to evaluate success. This will make a positive impression on the funder and will be valuable to your agency as you plan ongoing programs.

- After you receive corporate funding, be certain to ask the funder about their expectations concerning progress reports. Meet whatever dates are established, even if your project is not yet complete. Accurately describe the results, even if the program did not achieve the expected outcome. Honestly explain the cause of the shortfall and any plans for improvement.

CHAPTER 7
Budgets and Financial Statements

☞ The Importance of Budgets and Financial Information

Just as with proposals sent to private and family foundations, corporate proposals usually require inclusion of an agency's operating budget, as well as a budget for the project in need of funding. Some companies also require audited financial statements or the equivalent. Since corporations rarely fund an entire project, most companies also require an agency to indicate other funders committed to the project or their plans to raise the additional funds.

Budgets do not need to be complex, but they must be complete and accurate. Generally, the budgets of agencies requesting larger-than-average grants will be more rigorously reviewed than grassroots agencies requesting smaller amounts.

Similar to the proposal narrative, budgets should be simple and clear. Most corporations realize that the financial experience of nonprofits is limited, and so they do not require pages of budgetary detail and footnotes. In addition to being extremely difficult to read, complicated budgetary material is often very confusing.

It is important to realize that all employees in a corporate foundation are not experts in financial matters. It is true that the staff of some types of companies, such as banks, insurance companies and utilities, usually have more financial experience and they are more likely to conduct an in-depth, line-by-line review of a nonprofit's financials and budget items. Most corporate foundation managers, however, have backgrounds in human resources, nonprofit management or general management, and not in finance. Most managers will conduct a complete review of the budget as part of their funding decision, but they are more interested in the overall case presented by **all components** of the proposal.

Financials are considered to be only one aspect of the overall picture of an agency's capability. Corporate foundation managers also look for indications of a certain maturity and stability that is not always reflected in the non-profit's financials. As one manager said, "If a non-profit has been around for three years, but none of our local managers have ever heard of them, that's important information. It may be more important than a balanced budget."

Although a necessary part of a proposal, a detailed budget, by itself, is not a guarantee of approval of your funding request. A good budget supports and clarifies the other components of the proposal, which together form a complete document that effectively communicates your case.

Do not be too quick, however, to attach a hastily prepared budget to your proposal hoping that the reader will have no financial experience and your budget will be given only a cursory review. A majority of the companies interviewed indicated that a detailed review of budgets played an important role in their decision to fund. (See Figure 7.1.)

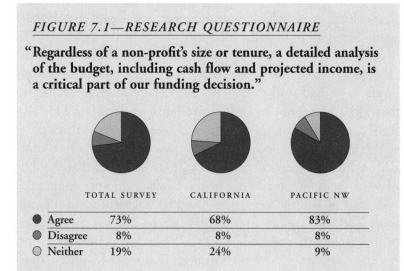

FIGURE 7.1—RESEARCH QUESTIONNAIRE

"Regardless of a non-profit's size or tenure, a detailed analysis of the budget, including cash flow and projected income, is a critical part of our funding decision."

		TOTAL SURVEY	CALIFORNIA	PACIFIC NW
●	Agree	73%	68%	83%
●	Disagree	8%	8%	8%
○	Neither	19%	24%	9%

Although the manager reading your proposal may not have a financial background, your budget will be completely analyzed. Regardless of their personal level of financial experience, the sheer volume of proposals that corporate foundation managers have reviewed over the years has developed their ability to easily identify a budget that appears inflated or expenses that seem under-reported.

Development of a complete and accurate budget may take some time, but it will add to the credibility of your proposal. Well-developed budgets ground your request in fact rather than conjecture. A complete budget also shows the level of planning and thought an agency has brought to the project. Companies are more likely to give their financial support to agencies whose budgets demonstrate thorough planning of the project's expenditures and revenue, and are less likely to fund agencies that appear unclear or indifferent about the project's finances.

☞ When Corporate Funders Review Your Budget

When reviewing a non-profit's budget, corporate managers look for signs of an agency's overall financial health. Although a review of individual line items is certainly part of their budgetary analysis, corporate managers are primarily interested in the total picture presented by the budget and financial statements. The following budgetary characteristics are considered to be general indicators of the health and viability of a non-profit's finances. These characteristics tend to be the focus of the corporate funder's review of a non-profit's budget and financials.

Indicators of Financial Health

1. Appropriateness of the line items.

2. Absence of significant debt.

3. Comprehensive listing of all expenses.

4. Cost-Effectiveness.

5. Realistic fund raising plans.

1. Appropriateness of line items.

When reviewing budgets, managers will not usually question individual line items unless something appears inconsistent, or if the line item seems to vary significantly from the normal costs usually associated with that particular type of expense. For example, after years of reviewing thousands of proposals that include mailing or printing costs, corporate managers are familiar with the average costs for these expenses. If your budget figures for these items differ significantly from the norm, the company will expect an explanation. Generally, it is best to include, beneath each line item in the budget, the formula used to calculate the expense. For example:

- Printing of Flyers $1,500 (3,000 flyers @ $.50 each)
- Mailing Expense $625 (2,500 pieces @ $.25 each)

Companies also review a budget to ensure that the types of expenses seem appropriate for the agency. For example, inclusion of large mailing expenses would be questionable if an agency has no community outreach program and has not included, in the proposal's narrative, a reason for excessive mailing costs.

2. Absence of significant debt.

In order to be viewed as a credible candidate for investment of the corporation's money, the agency's budgets and financial statements need to demonstrate overall financial stability. The existence of excessive debt provides a clue about the long-term viability of the agency. Non-profits in debt or in danger of bankruptcy will find it almost impossible to obtain corporate funding. Companies are reluctant to support non-profits with large debt because they believe that their grants are too small to prevent the inevitable demise of a non-profit in severe financial disarray. Supporting a severely financially stressed non-profit is considered a poor business decision since the impact of the corporate funding would be lost when the non-profit runs out of money and is forced to suspend its services. Unless there is a strong connection to a particular corporation, non-profits experiencing a financial crisis should seek funding elsewhere and approach corporations only after their finances have been stabilized.

If you decide to request corporate funding while in the midst of a financial crisis, do not camouflage your financial problem, but avoid making statements that reflect desperation. Instead, demonstrate control of the financial problem by clearly explaining the cause of the fiscal shortfall, and describing your plans and timetable for elimination of the problem. Indicate other sources of funding and describe contingency financial plans in the event you do not receive the company's money.

3. Comprehensive listing of all expenses.

Corporations expect budgets to simply make sense. They can usually identify those budgets that were hastily developed with minimal thought for the actual program costs, or budgets that were copied from another unrelated proposal. Companies want to see budgets that reflect careful planning and an anticipation of all direct and indirect project expenses. For example, non-profits requesting computers or other hardware from technology companies should include in their budget the expense for maintaining the equipment, as well as the expense related to training the staff to use the equipment.

4. Cost-Effectiveness.

Budgets are also reviewed to determine the cost-effectiveness of a program. For example, the budget for a program that provides tutoring services may be reviewed in terms of its cost per student. A program that provides meals for the needy may be evaluated in terms of its cost per meal. These ratios are useful when comparing the effectiveness of a number of agencies offering similar services. If all other factors are equal, the agency that delivers the service in the most cost-effective manner may be the most attractive candidate for corporate support. A non-profit agency's program may have demonstrated impact in a community, but if its program is judged to be more expensive than other similarly effective programs, the funding request may be denied and the grant given to the more cost-effective agency.

5. *Realistic fund raising plans.*

Only in rare cases will companies fund the total budget of a project, and so they are interested in the agency's plans to obtain the remainder of the needed funding. An agency's fund raising plans must appear viable and not exaggerated.

For example, despite optimistic claims that their proposal will be sent to another 15 foundations, a small non-profit with a total operating budget of only $125,000 is unlikely to interest enough additional funders in one year to support a completely new project that is budgeted for $100,000. Equally questionable are a non-profit's plans to support a new project by raising $100,000 in 12 months, from individual donors, when the budget indicates that individual donors contributed less than $5,000 during the previous year.

An agency's plans to raise additional funding must be realistic given its past history of raising funds and its current financial state. Overly optimistic fund raising plans can damage the credibility of a proposal, and can result in the agency being viewed as lacking experience and financial sophistication, which could ultimately result in denial of funds.

☞ Salaries, Fund Raising and Other Overhead Costs

Unlike many private foundations, the size of a non-profit's salaries was not a concern for most corporate funders. Only a few companies considered the size of salaries to be a major factor in their budgetary review. A few companies compare an agency's salaries to industry norms and they expect an explanation of any significant differences. Others were interested in the size of the Executive Director's salary in relationship to the rest of the staff. A significantly larger Executive Director's salary would require explanation. But generally, companies realize that the budgets of some non-profits, particularly those that are service-oriented, may have salaries as the largest expense item. It is still a good idea, however, to include an explanatory statement in your budget if the salaries of the staff in your agency are significantly higher than the norm.

There was no agreement on the acceptable size of overhead expense in a budget. Companies recognize the need for overhead expenses (office rental, utilities, etc.) in the day-to-day operation of a non-profit, although they obviously want to see as much of the budget as possible dedicated to actual program expenses. When asked for a specific overhead figure, there was no consensus among corporate funders. Responses concerning an acceptable overhead expense figure ranged from 15% to 40% of the operating budget. Acceptable fund raising expenses ranged from 10% to 20% of the operating budget. When reviewing the overhead expenses in budgets, companies seem more interested in what **makes sense for the agency,** rather than identifying a specific overhead percentage. Most were willing to consider larger overhead percentages if the agency could provide an acceptable reason.

However, before you decide to randomly add to your overhead spending, you should realize that overhead costs can be the deciding factor when companies review proposals from different agencies providing similar services. Extremely high overhead expenses will reduce the cost-effectiveness ratio of your service and perhaps cause your program to be judged as less effective than another similar agency.

☞ Red Flags in a Budget

When reviewing budgets, companies indicated that they looked for "red flags," which were defined as indicators of an agency's financial instability. The existence of red flags in an agency's budget might cause the funding request to be denied, unless explanations are included in the proposal document.

Red Flags in a Budget

1. Any appeals for emergency funds to keep the agency in business.

2. Large unexplained reserves or endowment.

3. Irregularities in the auditors' notes.

4. Math errors.

1. Any appeals for emergency funds to keep the agency in business.

Companies review the financial statements to ensure that the non-profit agency is reasonably solvent and not just surviving month-to-month. Companies want to support winning projects so that their grant dollars will have a positive impact in the community. Insolvent agencies are too risky an investment for most companies; therefore, companies avoid non-profits that seem desperately in need of financial support. As a rule, companies do not respond positively to pleas for emergency financial assistance; instead, preferring to fund more financially stable agencies.

Financials that reflect large liabilities, loans, payroll taxes payable or pending lawsuits are also a concern. Any liability that will come due in a few years will cause a company to research the non-profit further before approving a request for funding. If your agency has large liabilities or revenue shortfalls, the financial section of your proposal must include an explanation of your plans to retire this debt.

2. Large unexplained reserves or endowments.

Large reserves can also cause a company to question the need to fund a non-profit. If a non-profit has large amounts of funds in reserve, the belief is that the company's money is not needed. Some corporations believe their dollars will have more impact if given to a smaller agency with strong financials, but without a large budget surplus. If you do have large reserves indicated in your financial statements, be sure to include a statement explaining the need for the additional corporate funding.

During the interviews, some companies indicated that they would not fund endowments. They explained that since their company does not have an endowment, they see no reason for a non-profit to have an endowment. However, many non-profits have successfully utilized endowments to cover their operating expenses, and so I would not recommend ending this practice if it is successful for your agency. Including an explanation in the budget of the need and use of the endowment may be sufficient for the potential corporate funder.

3. Irregularities in the auditors' notes.

Almost all the companies indicated that they read the auditors' notes to the financial statements, looking for comments indicating any irregularities in the financials. Any anomalous factor should be clearly explained in the notes to the budget. Do not ignore the issue, hoping it will be overlooked by the funder. Explaining irregularities shows your agency's awareness and mastery of its financials. If the financial statements have not been audited, the company looks for some indication that accounting controls are in place.

4. Math errors.

Incorrect calculations were also mentioned as a cause for concern. While the inaccuracy may be nothing more than a simple math error, it could be interpreted as carelessness about finances. When creating a budget, double-check your math. Even if you use a software program to calculate the figures, recheck the work. An incorrect formula in the software program can inadvertently cause errors in the budget which will reflect poorly on your proposal.

☞ Asking for Funds

Asking for funding is very difficult for most non-profit agencies. Most non-profit staff and volunteers would rather do almost anything else than ask for money. Those that eventually do ask for funding usually try to complete the dreadful task as soon as possible. It is, therefore, not surprising that the actual funding request in a proposal is frequently given little thought by the non-profit. In fact, the amount of money you request from a company should be planned just as carefully as the rest of the proposal.

> **Simply asking for anything and hoping for something is not the best method of requesting corporate funding.**

There is no reason to be shy or apologize for your funding request. Remember, you are not begging for a hand-out. Your proposal documents a business transaction in which the company receives something of value in exchange for its financial support of your agency. Do not demand support, but be straightforward and clear in your request. Do not bury the funding request somewhere in the body of the proposal. Make the specific request in the summary section of a full proposal, or in the first paragraph of the letter of inquiry. Your proposal will flow more easily when the request is included at the beginning of the document and the supporting narrative follows.

Be certain to include a statement that requests a specific amount. You will not receive funding support if you do not actually ask for it. Do not imply your needs, use the actual words. Do not assume the company understands a veiled hint of a request. Companies do not want to be put in the position of having to figure out how much money is needed by a non-profit. For example, the following request can leave a company wondering what an agency is actually requesting:

• "Our AIDS prevention program needs financial help. We need at least $5,000 to continue our program for the rest of the year and we hope you can support us with a grant of some kind."

The following request is more specific and leaves no doubt about what requested:

- "We request a grant of $5,000 from ABC Company Foundation for mailing expenses associated with the community outreach component of our AIDS prevention program."

Avoid vague requests such as, "We would be happy with whatever you can afford," or "Whatever you think is best will be appreciated." This type of request can indicate an agency's unwillingness to take responsibility for its proposal and perhaps for its project. If the agency does not feel capable of asking for money for its program, companies may assume the agency is also uncomfortable with managing money. As a result, the company may make its investment elsewhere.

Also, you must indicate the manner in which the requested funding will be used—for general support, salaries, equipment, training, etc. Here again, a review of the company's guidelines is critical. The guidelines will indicate the areas which are not funded by the company. Be certain the company supports the type of activity that you need funded. Do not attempt to stretch the guidelines to fit your funding needs.

For example, if the guidelines indicate that the company supports educational programs and educational equipment, but does not support audio-visual equipment purchases, your request for a camera for a school project will be denied. Your project may be educational in nature, but the company does not fund audio-visual equipment, such as cameras.

If your request is for equipment, software or other in-kind support, be certain you have correctly identified the company's products before you request their in-kind support. Your request must be for a product made by that company and not for a product made by another company in a similar line of business. For example, do not request Macintosh® computers from Intel Corporation. Do not request software from a hardware company.

☞ Determining the Amount to Request

The amount you request must fit within the context of your agency's operating budget. Requests that seem inconsistent with the size of your operating budget may be denied. For example, a request for a grant of $10,000 from an agency with a total operating budget of $50,000 is suspect. Even if the company makes grants of this size, a request for 20% of the agency's entire operating budget will most likely be considered too high.

A common misconception is that if a company is interested in a program, but the non-profit requests an amount that is considered inappropriately large, the company will just give a smaller grant than what was requested. I've heard many non-profits say, "We'll just ask for $15,000 and if the company decides that's too much, they'll just give us less." Unfortunately, this is not always true.

While it is true that companies may award a grant that is smaller in size than the original request, this is usually due to budgetary pressures on the company. There may be insufficient funds available to provide the entire requested amount, but the company feels the proposed program is commendable and wants to make some kind of contribution. However, some company representatives indicated they might decline a proposal if it includes an inappropriately high request, or if the request exceeds the company's maximum funding levels. There are a number of reasons for this:

- First, a request that is inappropriately high may indicate that the non-profit did not do its homework and did not research the funding amount most appropriate for their proposal.

- Second, it may indicate an indifference toward finances and project planning.

- Third, the company may think that a smaller-sized grant will not have any significant impact on the project. Remember that companies rarely give funding for altruistic reasons alone. They want their financial support to make a difference in the community. The company may, instead, give their money to another agency that has requested a smaller amount because they believe their grant will have more of an impact with that agency. As one manager said:

> **"If a request is way out of line, it's easier to just deny it and not give a smaller gift. The smaller gift probably would not help that much anyway."**

When asked if non-profits should first call the company and ask for advice on the appropriate amount for a request, the companies disagreed in their responses. Some were willing to give input, while others felt it was the responsibility of the non-profit to determine the amount to be requested.

Usually, a company's guidelines will state the average grant size. You can also determine the size of the company's grants by requesting a list of grants awarded in the past, or by researching the company in a directory of corporate giving. (See Appendix 3 for corporate giving directories.)

If you are applying to the company for the first time, your request should not exceed the average grant. Do not be disappointed if you receive a grant below the average figure, since the average may be distorted by one or two large-sized grants. Agencies that already have a connection to the company, or that have received the company's support in the past, can request grants above the average amount.

In all cases, your request must make sense, given the size of your operating budget and your program's expenses. There is no need to spend an inordinate amount of time struggling over the correct amount to request. Research the company and consider your true funding needs. A good rule for first time requests is to ask for what you need, as long as it does not significantly exceed the average grant given by the company.

> **Ask for what you need, but do not assume that corporations have unlimited amounts of money to give away. As one manager said, "My company is not an ATM."**

In most situations, corporate grants are only for one year. Companies very rarely make multi-year grants in order to avoid creating a dependency on their funds. The few multi-year grants awarded each year are usually given to non-profit agencies that are well-known to the company and that have established relationships with them. First time applicants for funding should not request multi-year grants. Most companies are willing to consider funding programs for more than one year, but a separate proposal must be submitted and evaluated each year.

☞ **Providing Funding Options**

Most non-profit agencies request funding for a specific project, and such an approach is completely acceptable. However, a number of companies indicated their preference for **options** when non-profits request funding. Options are particularly attractive when the non-profit is applying for the first time to the company. When providing options, a non-profit describes a number of aspects of a program that require funding, and the company is given the choice of deciding which aspect of the program, or option, will be funded. This allows the company to choose to fund the component of a program most in alignment with their funding interests. Options give a company more latitude in their funding decision.

However, the use of funding options does not imply a loosening of financial control. Without careful planning, offering funding options to the company can appear to be more of an abdication of responsibility. The following is an example of a poorly worded funding option:

• "This project has many aspects requiring funding and we request a grant of $5,000 to be spent in any manner you feel is best."

Rather than offering specific options to the company, this request seems unfocused and unclear. It might be interpreted as a sign that the non-profit lacks control of its finances and is unsure of its own funding needs. Instead, the non-profit's funding request must be clear and specific. The following is an example of a more appropriate funding option:

• "We request a $5,000 grant from the ABC Company Foundation to be applied toward the training of counseling assistants for our multi-faceted family care program. If this aspect of the program does not meet the needs of the ABC Company Foundation, the $5,000 can be applied toward the purchase of consumable lab supplies for the program's immunization component, or for textbooks for the tutoring component of the program."

This request identifies a specific need for the funding, while also providing the company with a number of options. The company is given flexibility in its funding decision, while the non-profit retains control and accountability for the project's finances.

☞ Identifying Other Sources of Funding

The funding section of a proposal is more than a budget, financial statements and a request for support. Proposals should also identify the agency's plan for obtaining all the funding necessary for the program. This ensures the company that the non-profit has a diverse funding stream and is not relying on the company's funding alone to support the project. It also indicates that the non-profit intends to pursue the funding necessary to ensure continuation of the project after the corporate grant has been spent. This is an important detail, since most companies are unwilling to fund a project that appears to have little chance of surviving after the corporate funds are exhausted.

The larger the funding request, the more important it is to have other funders already committed. Although it is not necessary to have raised all the needed funds before requesting corporate support, you do need a credible plan to raise the remainder of the funds. This is commonly done through a listing of other funding sources, those already committed, those you plan to approach and those whose funding decisions are pending. Listing only the funders you intend to ask for funding does nothing to prove your financial stability and ability to actually implement the project.

Before you include a particular corporation or foundation on your list of companies that will be approached for funding, you must do your homework and research these funders for appropriateness. Merely listing names of a few foundations or corporations and entitling it "Potential Funders" is ineffective. If the company that receives your proposal knows those other funders and also knows that their funding interests do not match your program, your credibility will suffer and—reducing the likelihood that your agency will receive the company's funding.

The strongest proposals indicate other funding sources that have already committed to support your project. A listing of committed funders makes a more compelling case and demonstrates that the long-term viability of the project is not dependent upon receipt of one company's funds. It also provides a subtle psychological advantage that might entice other funders to also support the program. The reputation of the committed funders serves as a type of informal recommendation of your program. Listing a well-respected company as a committed supporter may cause other companies to look more favorably on your program, and perhaps decide to also provide support.

> The most effective list of funders includes a diverse base of support and shows that the project or agency is supported, not only by corporations and private foundations, but also by the agency's Board of Directors, memberships and individual contributions.

Companies reported being favorably impressed when non-profits included community foundations as committed funders, since those organizations are known for thoroughly researching a non-profit before approving a proposal request. Successful completion of a funding review done by a community foundation is considered, by many companies, to be an indication of the strength of the non-profit's program. Listing a community foundation as a committed funder becomes particularly effective when the non-profit seeking funding is unknown to the company.

Listing United Way as a funder can have both a positive and negative influence on your proposal. Some companies consider the funding reviews done by United Way to be very thorough and complete. United Way's support of your agency can be a positive factor similar to the support from community foundations. However, those companies that contribute to United Way as part of their corporate funding program will usually not fund non-profits already receiving United Way funds, since they believe the non-profit has already benefited from their company's charitable giving through United Way.

Corporations believe that donations from individuals are the only funding streams likely to increase over time and these donations can help to provide an ongoing, reliable funding base for non-profit agencies. Including individual donors on your list of other funding sources will demonstrate your financial savvy and understanding of the need to seek financial support from various sources.

Agencies supported primarily by government grants are considered risky by corporations, particularly in this climate of reduced government funding. There is a belief that government support will continue to decrease in the coming years, endangering the existence of the agencies that depend solely on the government for their funding. If your list of additional funders consists primarily of government grants, your chances of obtaining corporate support will be negatively impacted unless you include plans to reduce your dependency on the government.

Some companies, particularly retail chains, utilities, banks, and companies with strong competition in the local community, will frequently review a non-profit's list of corporate funders looking for names of their competitors. Some of these companies reported an unwillingness to fund a non-profit that is already funded by a competitor, although others were unaffected by funding from a competitor.

Do not be concerned about receiving funding from competing companies. Including in your proposal a complete list of the other funders you have already approached, and those you intend to ask for funding, is sufficient. Allow the company to decide if the presence of their competitors on your funding list is justification for denying your request.

☞ Corporations as the Lead Funder

The level of risk and uncertainty associated with new projects discourages most corporations from providing the "lead" or first grant to an agency or project. Without other committed funders, companies believe there is a strong possibility that the agency will not be able to raise the total funding required for the project, and the agency or the project will be forced to shut down or never be implemented at all. Companies do not want to invest in programs that are anything less than "winners," and so are more likely to support projects that have already received funding from other sources. (See Figure 7.2.)

Since corporations rarely have sufficient staff to research the effectiveness of proposed projects or new agencies, companies are more likely to withhold their funding until the new agency has attracted other reputable funders who may have the resources to complete the necessary investigation of their programs.

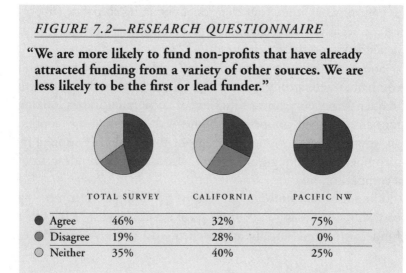

FIGURE 7.2—RESEARCH QUESTIONNAIRE

"We are more likely to fund non-profits that have already attracted funding from a variety of other sources. We are less likely to be the first or lead funder."

		TOTAL SURVEY	CALIFORNIA	PACIFIC NW
●	Agree	46%	32%	75%
●	Disagree	19%	28%	0%
○	Neither	35%	40%	25%

There were a few companies that were comfortable providing the lead gift, although they reported rarely receiving this type of request. These companies indicated that certain conditions were required to exist before they would consider providing the lead funding. For example, some companies would consider becoming the lead funder for a program only if they felt the proposal was very strong and the project was a very close match with their areas of interest. Other companies expressed a willingness to be the lead funder only if there was a matching funds component that would diminish some of the risk associated with providing the first funds for a project. This "challenge grant" arrangement would be contingent on the non-profit agency raising an identical amount from other sources. Some other companies would consider providing the lead funding for a new project developed by an established agency; an agency already well-known to the company. In this case, the relationship that existed previously between the company and the non-profit would alleviate some of the risk of lead funding. Some companies indicated a willingness to allow non-profits to use their corporate reputation and willingness to provide the lead funding as a way to attract other corporate funders. Again, this usually involved non-profits that had a previous relationship with the company.

Generally, non-profit agencies lacking a strong relationship with a company would be more successful approaching a company for a grant only after funding has first been obtained from other sources. As the data indicates, although a few corporations are willing to consider lead grants, the possibility of actually obtaining a corporate lead grant is remote.

☞ Implications and Recommendations

- Your proposal may be read by a manager who does not have extensive financial background. Be certain the financial section is clear and easy to follow. Although the budget should be an accurate and complete itemization of all expenses and income, do not complicate the information by adding long lists of line items and pages of complex footnotes.

- Do not try to hide line items that seem to differ from the norm, but instead include a short explanation.

- Use the financial section to illustrate your agency's financial stability. List funders already committed to the project and define your plans to secure additional funders.

- Your financial section should show responsibility, not desperation or confusion.

- Specifically ask for the funds you need. Avoid begging for "whatever you think is best."

- A new non-profit should first try to secure funding from a community foundation or a private foundation before requesting corporate funding.

- Cultivate a broad range of funders. Do not rely on one or two funders to support your entire program. Seek funding from individuals, as well as foundations and corporations.

- New non-profits should consider offering funding options to corporations. Offer several different components of one program as funding options, and allow the company to choose the option that best meets their interests. But do not allow the use of funding options to cause your proposal to become unfocused or unclear. Ultimately, if a company is interested in your program, but wants to fund a different component than the one you described, they will contact you.

CHAPTER 8
Additional Factors in the Funding Decision

Many corporate funding decisions are reached solely on the basis of the quality of the proposal and the degree of match between corporate goals and the work of the non-profit agency. However, increased demand for corporate financial support, combined with requests for larger amounts of money, has caused some corporations to consider more than the written proposal when reviewing agencies for funding.

The leadership of the board and staff is becoming increasingly important as companies look for the best investment for their charitable dollars. The capability of an agency's board and staff is considered a prime indicator of the agency's ability to make a measurable difference in the community. By giving their charitable dollars to well-managed non-profit agencies, companies believe their funding is more likely to be used effectively and their overall philanthropic program will have a greater impact.

Companies use a variety of methods to identify the level of leadership in a non-profit agency including: a review of the list of board members, interactions with the agency's Executive Director, discussions with other corporate funders and site visits.

☞ The Board of Directors

The composition of the non-profit's Board of Directors is one indicator of the agency's level of leadership. Your agency's credibility and its ability to make the changes outlined in your proposal is enhanced by a strong Board of Directors. In the past, the strongest boards were felt to be those that represented great wealth or access to wealth, or that included influential people. That type of board is still important, to some degree, to achieve the fund raising plans of non-profit agencies.

This "trophy board"—consisting of celebrities, wealthy individuals or high profile outsiders with only minimal knowledge of the issues—may be effective at sponsoring special fund raising events, but without a deeper involvement with the agency and the issues, this type of board will not contribute to the strength of your proposal.

This is particularly true in Southern California, where corporations are accustomed to receiving proposals listing Boards of Directors composed of entertainment industry celebrities. Companies believe that most celebrities listed as board members are actually only "lending" their name to an issue, and are not interested in participating in the ongoing activities of that non-profit agency. In contrast, the few celebrities who are known for their active support of an issue or an agency can add credibility to an agency's board list.

Those companies that use their philanthropic giving primarily as a way to create influence and goodwill are still primarily interested in supporting non-profit agencies with high profile, well-known board members. Many other companies, however, are becoming more interested in agencies whose boards of Directors reflect the demographic composition of the community and the clients they serve. A board that does not reflect the gender and ethnic mix of the community risks being perceived as separate from that community. These non-profit agencies may be considered unable to completely understand the climate of the community and, despite any past successes, may not be considered to be the best investment for a company looking to make a local community impact and influence community members. A board that includes community members is felt to have a better perspective of the community's real needs and is better able to assist in the design of programs that will have real impact on those needs.

Corporations also look favorably upon agencies that invite previous clients to become members of their board. The personal experiences of previous clients can help evaluate the effectiveness of the programs and ensure that the needs of the target population continue to be met. Programs that are designed with input from previous clients are perceived as having more of a chance for success than programs designed with minimal input from the community.

> **Those non-profit agencies that include members of the community or the target clientele on their board, and involve these members in the design and implementation of their programs, are considered to be more "in touch" with the community and are more powerful candidates for corporate funding.**

As more companies begin to consider their charitable giving to be an investment and not an altruistic donation, they are looking for boards that have the capability to manage that investment. In addition to an ethnically diverse mix of members, the most effective Boards of Directors include those whose members have the administrative skills needed to manage the non-profit agency. This is considered particularly important for small non-profits lacking trained staff members. An effective board includes professionals such as attorneys and tax accountants, or those able to obtain these skills for the non-profit. Board members should also possess skills and knowledge in the field in which the non-profit is operating. For example, if the goal of your non-profit is improvement of K-12 science curriculum, an effective board would include those with related skills such as teachers, scientists and curriculum experts.

☞ The Executive Director

The reputation of the Executive Director can have a strong influence on the outcome of the proposal. A respected Executive Director can alleviate some of the risk associated with funding a new project or a new non-profit agency, while an unknown or less-respected Executive Director can add to the funding risk. This is particularly true in the Pacific Northwest, where companies indicated they were familiar with the Executive Directors of most non-profits in the area and were most comfortable funding those agencies that were led by directors who were known to them.

This reliance on relationships can pose an obstacle for new agencies in that region, especially if their Executive Director is also new to the area and unknown to the funding community. Executive Directors who are unknown to the funder can use phone contacts, exposure in the community and in the local media, and site-visits to develop a rapport with the company representative, and demonstrate their leadership skills and ability to manage the agency. Non-profit agencies that hire Executive Directors from other non-profit agencies should recognize that when an Executive Director transfers from one agency to another, his reputation comes along with him, for better or for worse.

Corporations expect Executive Directors to be able to clearly and concisely describe the agency, its mission and goals. Executive Directors with rambling speaking styles should practice a succinct and clear explanation of the agency and its programs. Executive Directors should also be knowledgeable about the agency's financials, the plans to generate additional funds and contingency plans to support the program if the expected funding does not materialize.

Companies described the most effective Executive Directors as having the ability to articulate a vision of the future that generates excitement among those connected with the agency. These Executive Directors have a high level of knowledge about the issues and an intense commitment to make an impact in the field. They are unwilling to work in isolation and actively seek partnerships with other similar agencies. Strong Executive Directors are leaders who have innovative ideas and look for solutions to the larger issue, and not just their portion of the issue. For example, a strong Executive Director of a homeless shelter is not only interested in the one shelter program that she directs, she is also interested in finding solutions to the broader issue of homelessness.

Summary of the Characteristics of an Effective Executive Director

- Clearly and concisely describes the agency, its mission and goals.

- Articulates a vision of the future that generates excitement.

- Knowledgeable about the issues.

- Knowledgeable about the agency's financials and fund raising plans.

- Intense commitment to make an impact in the field.

- Seeks partnerships with other similar agencies.

- Seeks innovative solutions to the larger issue.

☞ Communication Among Corporate Funders

The amount of communication that occurs among corporate funders differs by geographic region. Although grantmaker associations exist in most large cities or regions, funders in the Pacific Northwest, more than corporate funders in other regions, reported frequent communication with peers in other companies. Personal relationships have developed among these managers over the years to the extent that the corporate funding community in the Pacific Northwest was described as "A collegial group, knowing each other a long time." These relationships are used to share information about non-profits and charitable giving issues. This affiliation among funders has resulted, at times, in companies agreeing to leverage their individual funds by forming a coalition of companies that, together, support a specific issue or non-profit agency.

The years of budget cutting, downsizing and the resultant personnel changes have loosened the ties among corporate funders in California, particularly those in the southern part of the state. Although some corporate funders still have close relationships with each other, there is not the same level of camaraderie among the funding community as a whole. Still, corporate grantmaker associations meet periodically to discuss specific charitable giving issues and collaborative funding programs have been successfully implemented.

In all regions, companies may contact each other in order to get input about a non-profit agency, but they rarely make a decision to accept or reject a proposal based solely on the information received from the other company. There is a recognition that many factors influence a company's funding decision and these factors may not impact all companies equally. The funding decision that is right for one company may be inappropriate for another.

Discussions among corporate peers about non-profit agencies provide another source of data to assist the corporate funder in the funding decision. These discussions are an exchange of factual information and are rarely judgmental in nature. These interactions assist a corporate funder who may be interested in a proposal from a non-profit, but who has some lingering reservations. Input from a peer also provides additional information to a funder who may not have the time or the staff necessary to make a site-visit and further research the non-profit.

Companies also use their relationships with other companies to facilitate funding of programs. For example, a corporate funder may consider a particular program to be of critical importance to the community, but they are reluctant to assume all the risk as the only funder. The company may attempt to interest other companies in the program and form a funding collaboration.

When listing the corporate funders supporting your program, non-profits should differentiate between those companies that have agreed to fund the project, and those that are still considering the proposal. You can never be certain when one company may call another to ask about their decision to fund your agency. Inaccurately identifying a company as a funder of your program can seriously damage your reputation with the entire corporate funding community in your area, for a long time.

☞ Site-Visits

Budgets cuts and personnel reductions have limited the ability of many companies to conduct site-visits of non-profit agencies. Some companies have compensated for these staff reductions by having employees conduct the site-visits. Also, employees who work as volunteers at non-profits are sometimes asked to provide "insider" input about the impact and capability of the non-profit agency. Many other companies now only have time to conduct site-visits after the funding decisions already have been made. Then, the visit is used to establish a closer relationship with the agency, or evaluate the impact of the funding.

If a company does visit your agency, the company representative will look for signs that the agency is well-run, fiscally sound and having a positive impact in the community. The company representative will try to determine the strength of the Executive Director by talking with the her about the program, but also by talking with staff, volunteers and clients. An observant company representative may ask only a few direct questions, since the impact of a strong Executive Director will be apparent in the words and actions of those around him.

While on a site-visit, a company representative may ask questions about the agency's mission, programs and future plans, and also review the mission statement, budget and financial statements. However, the most important information about the leadership of an agency is frequently gained through observations of ordinary day-to-day interactions and through casual conversation with staff, receptionists, volunteers and clients. For example, clues about the management of a non-profit are evident in the manner in which phones are answered and clients are greeted. Impolite phone technique or curt responses to a client's questions can indicate an indifference about the quality of service provided by the agency and a lack of involvement by the agency's leaders.

The physical appearance of the office is not usually of interest to a company representative, and there is no need to use your limited funds to make improvements to the building in order to impress the company. Offices should be orderly without piles of paper scattered across desks. Too much clutter can indicate a disorganized, unprofessional operation. However, an effort to significantly upgrade your office can backfire if it creates the impression that more money was spent on office refurbishment than on program supplies. Your building does not need to be new, but it should be clean and well maintained. Serious maintenance problems or safety hazards can dissuade a company from investing in your agency.

During a site-visit, company representatives look for subtle warning signs of an agency adrift. The following are examples of warning signs that indicate a possible failure of leadership, and could cause a company to reconsider its plans to fund a particular agency:

Warning Signs Indicating a Possible Failure of Leadership

- Most staff members possess only a superficial understanding of the issues or the problem the agency is addressing, or there is disagreement about the important issues.

- The staff is unable to articulate clear plans for the program in need of funding.

- Disagreement among staff members, or among staff and board members, about the mission and goals of the agency.

- Signs of frequent arguments between staff and volunteers, or indications that the number of volunteers is decreasing.

- Inconsistency between the agency's overall mission and its programs.

- Disagreements about the job responsibilities of individual staff members.

- A lack of clear measures of success; no way to determine how well the agency is meeting its objectives.

- A sense that no one seems to be in charge.

- Lethargic, unexcited, bored staff or volunteers.

Site-visits should not be intimidating or cause extreme stress. The company representatives who visit your agency want to have a pleasant, informative visit. They are not planning to be deceptive or cause discomfort. They are merely trying to get a sense of the agency's culture and its way of doing business. You can help ensure a successful visit by planning ahead. There is no need to make any changes in your normal operation or choreograph your actions in advance. The company wants to see your agency operating in a normal mode. They do not want a rehearsed performance, although they expect the agency to be prepared. The following suggestions can add to the professional appearance of your agency and help to ensure a successful site-visit:

☞ Tips for a Successful Site-Visit

- A staff member, usually the Executive Director or a board member, should assume responsibility for the site-visit—accompanying the visitors and answering any questions. This includes reviewing the proposal before the site-visit to ensure familiarity with the details in the event questions are asked.

- When the company representatives contact you to schedule a site-visit, ask if they are interested in observing any particular part of your program or if they would like to discuss any specific questions during the visit. You may not get any specific answers, but if you are able to determine their questions in advance, be sure to plan the day in such a way as to provide the information they are seeking.

- All staff members should be made aware of the visit and reassured that there is no need to be nervous. The company representatives will most likely be pleasant, and the visit will probably be interesting and informative. In fact, the staff should be proud that the company has decided to visit and observe their work.

- The staff members responsible for the program described in the proposal should be available to answer questions. They should have a comprehensive understanding of the program and be able to supply additional details that supplement the information contained in the proposal.

- All staff should be neatly dressed. There is no need to buy new clothes, but a messy appearance is inappropriate. It is important to realize that business people are accustomed to working with other business people. Neat attire gives a professional, business-like impression.

- Speak slowly, clearly and in complete sentences. Make eye contact when speaking.

- While no one should memorize lines, the staff should be prepared to explain their roles in the agency. It is also a good idea for staff to be familiar with the agency's mission statement and goals. No one will be asked to recite the mission statement, but the staff may be asked to explain the agency's goals, in their own words.

- Do not search for materials during the visit. Have copies of pertinent documents available such as: the agency's mission, budget and financial statements, list of board members, the agency's annual report if available, an artist's drawings of any planned construction and selected news clippings. Create a "press kit" for the company representative by including these documents in a plain folder or a folder with your agency's logo. This will add to the professional image of your agency. Be selective in including material in the folder; too much material will overload the reader and probably will not be read.

- Plan for opportunities to showcase your agency's work. You might create a display or arrange a short performance of your clients' work, or ask a few clients if they would be willing to discuss their personal experiences in your program with the company representatives.

    At the conclusion of a site-visit, send a short letter to the company representatives, thanking them for their interest in your agency. This simple sign of courtesy is noticed by the corporate funder and will help create a positive reputation for your agency. You may not be funded, but you will have developed the basis for a relationship with the company which will be beneficial when you reapply for funding the following year.

Be certain to follow-up with any suggestions offered by the company representative during the site-visit. For example, if the company representative suggests that you send certain material or submit a proposal on a different program, do so as soon as possible. If you delay submitting the requested material for months without an explanation, the proposal may be denied. Companies will be unwilling to support a non-profit that lacks basic business courtesy and is unable to respond to a simple request for information. Your chances for future funding may also be damaged if the company assumes that your lack of follow-up is not an isolated incident. It may be considered indicative of your agency's normal way of doing business and there may be a concern that your agency's indifferent attitude toward the company is also extended to your clients.

> **Those companies that utilize site-visits as part of their funding decision emphasized that a site-visit does not mean that funding is imminent. It is possible for a company to visit an agency, enjoy meeting the staff and yet, still decide to deny the funding request of that agency.**

A site-visit is only one aspect of the total funding decision. It is another step on the path toward obtaining corporate funding, but a site-visit is not a guarantee of funding. After a successful site-visit, it is not unusual for a non-profit agency to be denied funding. As one manager said, "Like any business transaction, you may like the people but still not buy what they're selling."

☞ Implications and Recommendations

- When attaching a list of your Board of Directors to your proposal, include each member's job title or connection to your agency. Use this as an opportunity to demonstrate the wide range of skills and leadership capability included on your board. Indicate board members who are current or previous clients of your agency, or employees of the company.

- When listing other sources of corporate funding, be certain to differentiate between corporate funding that is **committed** and corporate funding that is **pending.**

- Executive Directors should seek out opportunities to increase their exposure to the funding community. Speak about the issues at community events, cultivate media coverage and participate in community business networking forums.

- If a site-visit is requested by a corporate funder, prepare an informative day that will thoroughly acquaint the funder with your agency and its work. However, there is no need to spend a great deal of time creating a special show. The company representative will be interested in seeing the normal operation of your agency.

- Inform all staff members of a pending site-visit. Ensure the staff is adequately prepared to discuss their program, but do not require memorization of lines. Encourage the staff to be relaxed.

CHAPTER 9
Responding to the Funding Decision

☞ If Your Proposal is Accepted

If your proposal is successful and you receive a corporate grant, immediately contact the company and thank them for the gift. If you make the contact by phone, follow the call with a short written note signed by the Chairperson of your Board of Directors.

Normally, the letter from the company announcing the grant award will include the company's expectation about progress reports, use of the company's logo and general expectations about interaction with the company during the period of time covered by the grant. If this information is not received from the company, be sure to inquire about the company's requirements.

Also, be certain you understand the company's requirements regarding use of their corporate logo. Many companies have very formal procedures which must be followed before their logo can be displayed. They may have very precise directions concerning the color and size of the logo, type of font and the manner in which it is displayed. Do not assume that since you are using the logo to thank the company, you can disregard company directives concerning its use.

As discussed previously, most companies expect some type of evaluation or progress report detailing the result of their funding. Similar to their investments in stocks, companies are interested in the status of their investments in charitable programs and they want to be informed of the program's outcomes. A successful outcome can assist corporate foundation managers in justifying, to their superiors, the need to maintain or increase the size of the company's charitable giving budget.

Even if no formal report is required, it is a good idea to periodically send **short** news clippings or a **brief** report about the progress of the program that was funded. Do not inundate the manager with paper and phone calls, but remain in contact during the period that the grant is in use. As one manager said,

> "It's important to remain on our radar screen." Do not just take the grant money and disappear until the next funding cycle.

However, before sending any reports or news clippings, check with the company to determine if feedback is desired. A few companies indicated they did not want to receive any progress reports at all because they lacked sufficient time to read and process them. If the company does not want any reports, do not send anything! Ignoring the company's wishes and sending news clippings or reports because you felt they were interesting, will not be looked upon favorably and could damage future funding requests.

If your agency receives a grant from a company, it is expected that the company's money will be used as described in your proposal.

> If, after receiving the corporate grant, your agency is unable to generate the necessary additional funds and decides to terminate the project, the company must be informed. Do not assume the company will allow you to use the funding elsewhere.

Most companies will allow you to transfer their grant to another project, but they first expect you to inform them of the change in plans and formally request reapplication of the funds to another program.

After receiving a grant, you have an opportunity to develop a relationship with the company and perhaps interest the corporate foundation in increasing its support the following year. The most effective way to keep the company interested in your program is through simple demonstrations of your agency's impact. For example, you might invite the company representatives to a special performance by your clients, or conduct "funder breakfasts" and invite the company to participate, with civic leaders, in discussions about the impact of your project. The corporate foundation manager may be too busy to attend these types of events, but your effort will be positively noted.

After receiving a corporate grant, it is also important to consider the timing of subsequent requests for funding from the same company. Receiving an award of a corporate grant does not mean the company will become an unlimited source of funding for your agency.

> **Although a company may be willing to consider awarding your agency with another grant in the future, you can easily insult a company by asking for additional funding too soon after receiving their grant.**

For example, if your agency receives a corporate grant during the first quarter of a year, you might think it is acceptable to ask that company to purchase a table at your annual dinner held at the end of the year. However, most companies considered it inappropriate to request support for a special event during the same year that a grant was funded. In this situation, many of the companies felt that they should receive a free invitation to the dinner in recognition of their grant. A good guideline is to avoid requests for any additional funding during the same year that a grant is received from a company.

☞ If Your Proposal is Denied

Companies generally try to be equitable and thorough in their review of proposals. Many of the corporate foundation managers have an empathy for the work of non-profits, resulting from their own previous employment in the non-profit sector, or from their years interacting with non-profit agencies. The company representatives would like to be able to approve every proposal and they do not get pleasure from denying a funding request.

But proposals do get rejected. If your agency fails to receive funding, do not assume that you did something wrong during the site-visit or that your proposal was inadequate. The denial of the proposal is not necessarily a rejection of your skills as a writer. It also is not necessarily a judgment of the value of your agency. Not every good program will receive corporate funding. As one manager said,

> **"A denial letter is only a rejection of the request, it is not a rejection of the agency."**

Your proposal may be well-written, aligned with the company's guidelines and meet a community need, and yet you may still be denied funding. In fact, non-profit agencies, particularly newly-established agencies, should expect to receive a few rejections before their program is funded.

The nature of business demands that corporations strive to be recognized as the best in their field, and corporations bring this philosophy to their charitable giving program. Companies focus their charitable support in areas where they have expertise, where they understand the issue and where they believe their charitable giving program will have the biggest impact possible. As a result, their grant may be awarded to another agency, even though your agency is very effective in its particular field.

An unwillingness to fund your program is also not an indication that the company is irresponsible or unconcerned about social issues. No corporation can fund all non-profit programs and many effective, important programs will not receive corporate support. Although they may not have funded your program, the company may still be very involved in other important charitable issues.

During the interviews, many corporations spoke of the evolution of their charitable giving programs. As companies learn more about an issue, they tend to refine their grantmaking so their funding has a greater impact on the issue. For example, one company described its initial involvement with AIDS as little more than buying t-shirts for employees participating in an AIDS Awareness Day Walk. Over time, the company learned more about the AIDS issue, its impact on the community and on the company's employees. Years later, this company has become very involved in the issue, and contributes significant sums of money to agencies serving victims of AIDS and AIDS research programs. Therefore, the company that denied your funding request this year, may decide to fund your program in another year or two, after their understanding and interest in the issue increases.

Do not allow a denial of your proposal cause you to stop seeking corporate funding. Perhaps an earlier submission by your agency the following year will be a winner. Maybe another agency's project, funded by the company, will experience difficulty and will not be funded the following year, potentially freeing money to support your program. You might be more successful submitting a proposal for a different program to the same company the next year. You might also find, through research, that your proposal is a better fit with the interests of a different corporation or private foundation. Continue to research corporate giving programs and you will eventually find a successful match.

☞ The Most Common Reasons for Denying a Proposal

It is difficult to identify the specific reason that a proposal was denied. It may have been an exceptional year for proposals and many excellent proposals were received by the company, while at the same time the corporate charitable funding budget was reduced. Your proposal may have been considered to be very good, but other agencies had more positive variables. Maybe your proposal was the victim of poor timing, and the funding had been exhausted by the time your proposal was received.

Ultimately, deciding which proposals to fund and which to deny is a judgment call. Any of the factors identified in the previous chapters can influence the final decision and, since decisions are made by people and not by machines, there are numerous unconscious factors that also contribute to the funding decision.

When asked the most common reason for denial of funding, companies cited the following reasons, listed in the order of frequency:

Most Common Reasons for Denying a Funding Request

1. Guidelines were not followed.
The proposal was submitted even though the guidelines state that the issue or activity is not funded by the company.

2. Geographic preferences were disregarded.
The non-profit is located outside of the geographic region funded by the company.

3. Budget limitations.
The company's budget for charitable giving was exhausted before the end of the funding cycle. No money was available to fund any additional programs, regardless of their merit.

4. Competition
A similar project, submitted by another non-profit, was considered to be a better investment for the company. It was a better fit with the company's interests.

☞ Getting Input from a Company After Your Proposal Has Been Denied

Receiving a rejection of a proposal that took so much time to write can be disappointing. If you wrote the document, allow yourself some time to feel the disappointment, but do not become completely disheartened. After a little investigation and some edits to your document, you may still be able to secure funding for your program.

Regardless of whether you decide to reapply to the same company or to another funder, your actions will be more effective if you use the first few days after receiving a rejection letter to gain as much information as possible about the reasons for the rejection and ways to improve the proposal document. The best way to obtain information about your proposal is by contacting the funder directly or by carefully reading the denial letter.

1. Calling the company for input.

Companies were mixed in their willingness to accept calls from non-profits interested in discussing a rejected proposal. Not surprisingly, companies with larger staff sizes were most willing to give advice to non-profits. The company representatives use these calls to suggest ways the agency could improve their proposal, as well as to discourage agencies from resubmitting proposals for unacceptable projects. The company representatives felt their candor during these calls saved the non-profit the time of sending a proposal the following year that would also be denied. Most companies, however, said they rarely receive calls from non-profits requesting advice about a rejected proposal.

Other companies were reluctant to accept calls to discuss a rejected proposal because of the potential for awkwardness and defensiveness. Some managers compared the question, "Why didn't you fund my program?" to the question, "Why didn't you hire me?" Both can be equally difficult to answer. Corporate managers recognized the frustration that results from receiving a rejection letter, but they commented that it is also frustrating to try to give honest, constructive advice without hurting someone's feelings.

As a result, some companies are reluctant to identify the exact reason for a denial, and instead, tend to give a general response to requests for more information about a rejection. Experience has shown these corporations that many non-profit agencies have difficulty being told the truth about a rejected proposal and many will try to argue with the company representative. Many companies believe that while non-profit agencies may ask for input, they really do not want to be told that their proposal was rejected because of concerns about the capability of your staff, your financial stability, your chances of surviving into the future, your lack of competitiveness with similar agencies or because your proposal was unclear and full of typos. It is much easier to be told something nebulous such as, "There were so many qualified candidates, we had a difficult time choosing." Vague responses like this may make you feel better, but they do nothing to help you improve your proposal for the next submission.

The truth is not always an easy thing to hear and yet if you are seriously interested in attracting corporate support, you must be willing to listen, without comment, to the candid input from the corporate representative.

It is natural to feel defensive when someone critiques your work, but try to control your emotions during this interaction. The company representative is more likely to be straightforward in her response if she senses that you are actually interested in getting advice and not just looking for an argument.

If you decide to contact a corporate funder to request advice about your proposal, do so as soon as possible after receiving the letter of rejection. If you wait too long your proposal may be discarded and then, even if the funder is willing to talk, she may not remember your document clearly enough to provide any helpful information.

When contacting corporate funders, remember to value their time. Make your call short, ask only a few questions and most importantly, remain calm. Always end the call by thanking them for their time. Be polite but specific about what you want. Do not waste time with small talk. Corporate managers appreciate callers who get to the point quickly by using a statement such as, "We appreciate your consideration of our proposal and I am calling to ask if you could give me some feedback about how the proposal can be improved." If the funder is available to speak with you, the following are examples of specific questions you might ask:

- Was there anything about the way the proposal was written that caused a problem for you?

- Do you have any specific suggestions for improving this proposal?

- Is there a chance that you might be interested in this project next year? Would you suggest we upgrade the proposal and then resubmit it next year, or submit a request for a different program? (Be prepared to **briefly** explain one or two other programs.)

- If the funder indicates that your project is beyond the boundaries of their guidelines, do not argue. You can, however, ask if you could be referred you to another corporation that might be more interested in your project.

Clarify any point that the manager appears to have misunderstood, but do it professionally. Avoid comments such as, "But that's not what we meant. You read it wrong." Instead, use less volatile phrasing such as, "I guess we weren't clear about that in the proposal. What we really meant to convey was...." Remember, if the manager misunderstood the proposal, it was because the proposal lacked clarity. It's too late to make changes for this submission, but you can use this information to rewrite the confusing sections before you submit the proposal to another funder.

The responses that you receive from a call to a corporate funder may sound a little harsher than you would like, but the manager is just trying to help. The managers are not required to respond to your requests for suggestions, yet they can provide valuable tips for improving the overall quality of your document. During the call, take advantage of the manager's knowledge and experience, and his willingness to speak with you. Listen, take notes and calmly ask for clarification if you do not understand a specific comment. The suggestions given to you during that call may result in acceptance of the next proposal sent to this company or to another funder.

If the funder is reluctant to provide the specific information you want, do not try to apply pressure. Doing so may sabotage your future prospects of getting funded. Merely thank the staff person and end the call. The call may not have been successful, but congratulate yourself for making the effort.

If your calls to the funder are not returned, or the manager is too busy to answer your questions, try sending a **short** letter asking for information. Begin the letter by thanking them for considering your proposal, and then ask for input. Even if the manager is unable to respond, your attempts to follow-up will be positively noted.

Unless your issue is completely beyond the scope of their guidelines, rarely will funders discourage you from reapplying for a grant the following year. They may, however, hint or imply that your project is unlikely to be funded. When calling for advice about a rejected proposal, listen to the tone of the call. If the funder is not very positive about your proposal and does not encourage you to reapply, it may be a good idea to look elsewhere for corporate support.

2. Finding advice in a letter of denial.

Fewer and fewer companies have sufficient staff to respond to phone calls requesting more information about a rejected proposal. A combination of factors, including reductions in the size of foundation staffs, increases in the volume of proposals received by the company, and additions to the job responsibilities of corporate giving managers, leave little time for responses to phone inquiries. Even those companies that, in the past, routinely responded to calls from non-profit agencies inquiring about a denied proposal, are finding less time to do so now. These managers now rely on a letter to communicate to the non-profit the reasons for the rejection of a proposal.

Some companies will simply send form letters with minimal explanation when rejecting proposals from agencies that obviously did not follow the guidelines. If non-profits do not take the time to read and follow their guidelines, companies see no need to take the time to provide anything more than a form letter of rejection. These letters can be identified by their brevity and lack of specific information. For example, "We received your proposal for support from ABC Company's foundation. Since we received so many worthy proposals, we are unfortunately unable to fund your program." It is evident from this type of letter that the company is not interested in your particular program and resubmission of the proposal for the same program would probably be futile without further research into the company's giving interests.

More detailed letters are frequently sent to agencies that met the guidelines, but were denied for other reasons. These letters might identify a more specific reason for the denial, such as the corporate funding budget was exhausted, or the competition was particularly intense and funding was given to other more competitive agencies. If your agency receives this type of letter, resubmission to the company is a possibility. A call or letter to the funder requesting additional information may help you to make upgrades and write a stronger proposal for the following year.

☞ Resubmitting a Proposal

If you decide to resubmit your proposal the following year, do not send the exact same document. Add updated information and clarify any vague sections. If you are not certain about the effectiveness of sending a proposal the following year, closely review the company's guidelines. If you honestly believe your program meets the guidelines, resubmit the upgraded proposal. If your agency has another program, which is a stronger match with the company's interests, submit a proposal for that program instead. If you are rejected a second time, consider pursuing a different corporate funder.

Companies differ in their policies concerning application for additional funding after your proposal has been approved and your agency received a grant. Some companies permit an agency to reapply the following year, others require a wait of a few years before another proposal can be submitted. Very few companies will support a non-profit indefinitely, regardless of the impact of the agency's programs. Companies are very reluctant to foster a dependency on their funding and, eventually, expect all agencies to seek funding elsewhere.

☞ Implications and Recommendations: A Summary of Mistakes Made by Non-Profits Seeking Corporate Funding

In addition to the four major reasons for denying a proposal listed above, corporate funders also cited the following common mistakes made by non-profit agencies submitting proposals. These errors may not cause your proposal to be immediately denied, but they will detract from the overall impact of your document and will weaken your chances of competing with other agencies for the company's support. Most of these mistakes have been mentioned in previous chapters and they are summarized here to provide a quick check-list that can be easily reviewed as you develop a proposal.

Common Proposal Errors

- Submitting an unprofessional package—an incomplete application, misspellings, mistakes in the manager's name or the company's name.

- Asking for unreasonably large sums of money—much higher than the average given by the company—or neglecting to ask for a specific amount, and instead, vaguely asking for "any kind" of help.

- Presenting a document that reflects a lack of understanding of the type of business the company is in.

- Assuming that personal connections and relationships with influential people will compensate for a poor quality proposal or a program that is of no interest to the company.

- Arguing with the company representative when told your program does not meet the company's guidelines.

- Allowing feelings of intimidation and fear of big corporations cause the non-profit to avoid pursuing opportunities to develop personal connections within the company or its local offices and branches.

- A fear of talking to the funder and asking pertinent questions that would help in the development of the proposal.

- Trying to manipulate the funder by pursuing the support of rival companies and then appealing to the company's sense of competition.

- Inaccurate listing of other committed funders.

- Relying too heavily on corporate support because of an unrealistic expectation that corporate funding will compensate for diminished government support, or an inaccurate belief that corporations have unlimited sources of wealth and can afford to support all charitable causes.

- Failing to pursue funding from individuals, as well as from foundations and corporations.

- Believing the more information included in a proposal, the stronger its chances of being funded.

- Using an expensive overnight mail delivery service to meet a deadline.

- After receiving a grant, failing to inquire about the company's requirements for follow-up, such as the company's expectation for recognition of their gift, the proper use of the company's logo, the type and frequency of progress reports.

- Inability to present the project, verbally or in writing, in a clear, concise manner.

- Unprofessional presentation during a site-visit.

- Beginning new projects that are unrelated or only loosely related to the agency's mission in an attempt to be eligible for a specific type of grant.

- Failure to remain aware of changes in the needs of the community or changes in the demographic make-up of your clients.

- Calling for status only one week after submitting a proposal.

- Assuming the jargon commonly used in your agency will be easily understood by the reader.

- Assuming corporations will fund any project if they are offered appropriate public relations opportunities. Failing to understand that public relations is the responsibility of the marketing department, not the corporate foundation.

- Inaccurately categorizing informal interactions between agencies as formal partnerships in order to qualify for grants that require coalitions.

- Failing to determine if any volunteers or clients of the agency are employees of the company. Failing to take advantage of funding from corporate matching gift programs.

- Failing to thank the company for a grant.

- Failing to realize that a **geographic preference** listed in the guidelines indicates that proposals from those locations are given priority over proposals from all other locations.

- Missing due dates and attempting to have the proposal accepted anyway.

- Expressing anger at the corporation or making derogatory comments about the company to other funders after receiving a smaller-sized grant than was expected or after a funding request is rejected.

- Poorly scheduling your requests for support. For example, asking a corporation to buy a table at special event a few weeks after receiving a grant from that company.

- Expressing an unrealistic view of the non-profit's place in the community by assuming that no other agency is addressing the same problem or any other aspect of the same problem.

- Trying to solve problems in isolation, without the cooperation of other agencies. An unrealistic belief that one agency alone can solve the major issues confronting our society.

CHAPTER 10
A Summary of Tips to Improve Your Proposal

☞ The Professional Approach to Corporate Funders

Corporations consider their charitable giving to be an investment in the community and corporations do not invest their dollars recklessly. The money that is used to support non-profit programs is money that is not turned into profits for shareholders. Companies must be able to demonstrate the sound, underlying business reasons for their charitable investments, or risk the disapproval of the shareholders. Companies, therefore, fund those non-profits that they have determined to be good business investments. Your role, as a non-profit agency seeking corporate funding, is to demonstrate that your agency is a sound investment.

Although the process of seeking corporate funding can be intimidating to non-profit agencies unfamiliar with the world of business, it is not as complicated as it may initially seem. You really only need to identify the reasons for a company's corporate charitable giving and their areas of funding interest. Once you determine a match between your company's work and the corporate funder's interests, you then must understand and utilize the rules for interacting in the business world. Notice I used the word "company" to describe your non-profit agency. If you are to successfully navigate around the world of business, begin to think of your agency as a business. This means your interactions must be professional and confident, and you must use terminology familiar to business people.

To connect with corporations and attract their investment, non-profits need to interact with companies in the business manner that is most familiar to them. All your written and spoken communications must be professional, brief and to the point. The focus should be on facts. Including some emotion in a proposal is fine, but avoid filling the document with heart wrenching tales and anecdotal comments. Properly used, drama and emotion can increase a proposal's readability, but overused, it can make a fine project seem amateurish and untested.

When requesting financial support, you are asking a company to enter into a partnership with your agency in the creation of a solution to a particular issue. Your communications must demonstrate that your agency will be a capable partner and a successful investment. This is done with clear and concise facts, plans and outcomes.

☞ Recognizing the Value of Your Work

As a non-profit agency, it is important to recognize your power and importance in the community. You are experimenting with innovative solutions to critical environmental, social, educational, health care and family problems. You are engaged in finding answers to important social issues that have, to date, eluded many of the finest minds in the public and private sector.

The non-profit sector has a great ability to influence. Non-profit agencies speak for many in the community. Non-profits are supported by clients and donors who recognize and respect the value of the services they provide. These same people, your donors and clients, are courted by corporations looking to attract new customers and markets for their products and services. Corporations want to link their company name with the good name and reputation of non-profit agencies engaged in exceptional work in the community, and so the successful non-profit agency is an attractive investment for companies seeking to sway a particular customer set or constituency.

Regardless of whether a company's charitable giving is due to an honest desire to positively impact social issues, or for less lofty reasons such as public relations, employee motivation or increasing sales, more and more companies are beginning to see the advantage of developing partnerships with non-profit agencies. Charitable giving programs are frequently a strategic part of a company's overall business plan. Many companies want to be seen as supporting social issues of importance to consumers and are, therefore, actively seeking effective non-profit agencies to endorse.

When seeking funding from a corporation, non-profits should recognize the value they bring to the transaction. The non-profit is requesting financial support, but at the same time, the non-profit is also offering the corporations something of value.

> **Successful non-profit agencies identify the value they offer the corporation, and then they enter all transactions with the company with a professional, business-like attitude.**

You can capitalize on the corporate desire to partner with non-profit agencies by adopting a professional demeanor in all interactions with companies. It's understandable that some non-profit staff members feel nervous and uncomfortable even thinking about discussing their program with a corporate foundation manager, or overwhelmed when considering writing a corporate proposal. Yet, through proper preparation and research, non-profit agencies can successfully attract corporate financial support.

☞ Seeking Corporate Funding: A Summary of Suggestions

When asked to give suggestions to non-profit agencies seeking corporate financial support, all companies spoke of **"doing your homework,"** meaning that you must thoroughly research the company before sending a proposal. Do not send a "cold" proposal to a company. Avoid the mistaken belief that you have a connection with a company simply because you use their products. Do not assume the company will fund any good cause because they have an impressive bottom line and seem to have unlimited funds.

Instead, research the company through its annual report and foundation guidelines, its web site, newspapers and periodicals, lists of previous grants and informal talks with employees. Learn all you can about the company, its areas of funding and emphasis, its culture and values and the issues of strategic interest to the company. Find a reason to connect your agency's issue with the corporation. The amount of time a non-profit has put into researching a company will be reflected in the quality of the proposal. Company representatives appreciate this extra effort.

If you do not meet the guidelines or interest areas of the company, do not apply for a grant. Your proposal will be in competition with hundreds of other proposals that **are in alignment** with the guidelines. You do not have a chance of receiving a grant if your agency is beyond the scope of the company's interests. Be honest with yourself about your agency's connection to the company's guidelines. Do not try to convince yourself that there is a fit when none exists.

If you disapprove of the company's politics or business practices, do not apply for financial support. If you want to protest a company, do so. However, never mix protesting with fund raising. Veiled threats to boycott a store or "leak" negative information to the media unless funding is received, are never successful. Companies do not respond to extortion. They do respond to customer complaints and most are willing to listen to a calm discussion of concerns, but this is separate from their grantmaking process. If you attempt to use extortion to force a company to provide financial support, your actions will not only be unsuccessful, but illegal and unethical as well.

Corporate foundation managers and corporate giving managers want non-profits to be successful. Although they do not have the funds to approve every proposal, most want to help non-profit agencies create as good a proposal as possible. All the managers I interviewed had suggestions for non-profits considering applying for corporate funding. The following is a summary of those suggestions:

Tips to Improve Your Proposal

- *Project confidence.*

  The more you can communicate the feeling that you will be successful, the more likely your chances of getting a company's support. All companies want to invest in a program that they feel will be successful.

- *Non-profits should consider themselves a business, even if they do not make a profit.*

  When approaching companies, you will be interacting with people who are most familiar with the business model. Describe your agency and program in terms familiar to business people. Speak to the quality of your service, the satisfaction of your clients (customers), the capability of your employees, the objectives of your projects and the measures of your success.

- *Follow the company's requirements for the initial contact.*

  Some companies require a phone call or letter of inquiry to pre-screen your request, while others prefer a full proposal. The preferred method of initial contact will be indicated in the guidelines. If you make a call, value the manager's time. Be prepared with a concise summary of your program. Do not ask questions that are already answered in the guidelines. The first call can be frightening, so practice your phone skills first. Write down what you plan to say in the event you get tongue-tied. A good phone call can positively impact your proposal, but you can hurt your chances of being funded if you cannot concisely communicate the program on the phone.

- *Ask about the company's funding cycle.*

  If funding is on a calendar year, submit the proposal during the first six months of the year. If you wait until the end of the year, all the funding for the year may have already been allocated. If there are deadlines, submit the proposal a few weeks before the deadline.

Time your submission of the proposal to ensure the company has sufficient time to review it before the funds are needed by your agency. Some companies require six months to make a funding decision. Do not apply for funding of a project that is scheduled to be completed before a funding decision is made.

- *Be clear and concise.*

Many times the corporate decision-maker will only see a summary of your proposal, written by their staff member. Ensure that your major points will be included in the summary by providing clear, concise statements. Do not ramble or you will lose the reader's interest. Check and recheck spelling, grammar and the spelling of the company's name. A proposal is similar to a resume. It doesn't have to be perfect, but typos and lack of clarity will reflect poorly on the agency.

Do not send videos. If a video is available and it was funded through a donation, mention it in the narrative. If the company is interested, they will ask to see it. If you spent money to create a video, its best not to mention it unless the company requests additional information. The company may wonder why you felt creation of a video was a necessary expense.

- *The proposal should look easy to read.*

Avoid "walls of words." Use standard size fonts and margins. Bullet items wherever possible. Put the important information at the beginning of the proposal. Your proposal may be the fifteenth proposal read by the manager that day. Make it easy to read.

- *Demonstrate your knowledge of the community.*

Show partnerships and collaborations with community groups. Demonstrate your awareness of the work of other similar agencies. Use your proposal to educate the funder about the need for your program.

- ***Show your uniqueness.***

  Always indicate your niche. If you are the only provider of the service indicate the reasons the service is needed. If the service is also provided by other agencies, provide data demonstrating that your agency is the best provider of the service, but do not belittle other agencies. Do not assume that a company that has funded other agencies similar to yours will want to fund your agency. Answer the question, "Why should they fund your agency also?"

- ***Specifically indicate the amount requested.***

  Never apply in panic. Avoid desperate pleas for funding. Request a specific amount. Avoid statements such as "We are in great need and can use anything you can give."

- ***Avoid jargon.***

  The words may be familiar to you because you work in the field everyday, but they may be unknown to the corporate manager reading your proposal. Do not assume everyone is familiar with the specialized, organizational terms commonly used by your agency. The proposal should be understood without the use of a dictionary.

- ***Attend "meet the funder" meetings.***

  Companies realize that requesting charitable support can be a complicated, time-consuming process and may pose a drain on the limited resources of non-profit agencies, and so many companies are trying to simplify the proposal process. Many now require a short letter of inquiry instead of a proposal, and they post their guidelines on the internet. Many are becoming more visible to the non-profit community by attending events like "Meet the Funders Days."

  Non-profits should take advantage of this opportunity to talk informally with corporate funders. It is a great way to learn about changes in the company's funding program and, more importantly, it is an opportunity to meet those responsible for evaluating your proposal. Arrive at these functions prepared with a 30 second explanation of your agency and use it to introduce yourself to the company representative. This may seem a little awkward at first, but it gets easier after you attend a few of these functions. In most cases, the company representatives will be very willing to meet you, hear a **little** about your agency and answer any questions. If possible, review the corporate foundation's guidelines before the event in order to avoid asking questions already answered in the guidelines. You may impress the corporate representative with your level of preparation by asking for clarification of a point you read in the guidelines.

- *Indicate the names of employees or community leaders involved with your program.*

  Companies cannot fund every program that involves their employees, but many times programs involving employees, as clients or as volunteers, will get priority consideration. Companies interested in using their charitable giving to attract influence will be interested in a list of community leaders supporting your program.

- *Do not "chase money" by inventing new programs simply to meet the guidelines.*

  These new programs will be a serious drag on your budget after the corporate grant is spent. Request funding for existing programs or for new programs that are part of your agency's plan for growth. Companies usually like to support projects and not operating expenses, although a non-profit can sometimes get some support for their operating budget by allocating some administrative expense to the project.

- *For small grants, consider contacting a company's local branches or offices.*

  Local branches may provide your agency with small grants or donations of their products for your special events, through their marketing budgets, in exchange for local media exposure.

- *List achievable, realistic goals and objectives.*

  Goals and objectives should indicate the outcomes and the changes in behavior expected from your program, not just the process you will use.

- *Show financial stability by listing other funders.*

  Show funds already received or your plans to raise additional funds. It is more compelling to see a comprehensive plan for raising all the needed funds, including funders already committed to the project, instead of merely a list of foundations that will receive your proposal.

- *Do not be defensive or judgmental.*

  Consider all interactions with a company to be an opportunity to acquire additional information about the company and their perception of your proposal. If the company's perceptions about your agency or project are incorrect, do not become defensive or angry. The company may be wrong; however, it is their perception of your program and perceptions often form the basis for our reality. Instead, calmly clarify the misunderstanding.

  The less defensive you are, the more useful information you can get from the company. Questions such as "Why didn't you fund us?" or "Your Vice-President is on our board, why wasn't that enough?" will be met with innocuous responses such as "We had so many good proposals, it was impossible to fund them all." You are more likely to get valuable assistance with questions such as "How can I improve this proposal?"

- *Show a diverse funding stream.*

  A non-profit's financials are more effective when funding comes from a variety of sources. Investigate matching gift programs, cultivate individual donors, as well as private and other corporate foundations.

- *Show your measures of success.*

  Companies are very familiar with evaluations of project outcomes and will be favorably impressed with your focus on measuring success. An elaborate evaluation plan is not necessary, but there is a growing expectation that non-profits develop a method to determine if the program and the company's money had a successful impact.

- *Market your agency and your agency's impact.*

  Do not assume companies are familiar with your agency. Find ways to spotlight your agency and its accomplishments—indicate your agency's accomplishments, include testimonials from clients and describe the expertise of your staff and board.

- *Do not pressure a company.*

  Corporations do not respond well to veiled threats of extortion. Threatening boycotts of stores and products, or attempts to elicit feelings of guilt from staff for denying your funding request are ineffective ways of raising corporate funds. Equally ineffective is assuming your agency is entitled to a grant because you or your clients use the company's products or have accounts at the company's branches.

- *Send the proposal to the proper person.*

  Do not bypass the funding process by sending the proposal to an executive or the spouse of an executive. It will just be rerouted to the proper staff member, most likely, without the executive ever seeing it. If possible, call and ask for the name of the person to whom the proposal should be addressed. Be sure the name is correctly spelled.

- *Follow-up is fine if timed correctly.*

  Calling to determine the status of your proposal is a good way to stay connected with a company and might remind the funder to contact the proposal review team to determine the status of the document. However, calling only one week after submission can be annoying. Give the company at least a month to review your proposal before calling for status. Also, you should recognize that one result of corporate downsizing is the inability of foundation managers to return calls as quickly as they once did. If your call is not returned within 24 hours, give the manager another day or two before calling and leaving a second message. Your understanding will be appreciated. If the guidelines indicate that calls are not accepted, do not call!

- ***Corporate funders are people, too.***

Corporate funding managers are paid to decide who should be funded and who should not. Their decisions are bounded by their corporation's goals and guidelines. The corporate managers can only approve funding to those agencies that best meet the company's criteria. Getting angry or arguing with the manager because your proposal did not get the reception you had hoped is a waste of time and energy. Also, you may alienate the manager so much that you might damage future chances of funding. There is no need to disguise your disappointment after receiving a rejection, but do not focus your frustration on the manager.

I realize that there are a few corporate funding managers who are unfriendly. If you encounter a rude funder, remain polite and try to get the information you need. Then quickly end the interaction and move on. Do not take the interaction personally. It might just have been a bad day for the manager.

- ***Watch out for assumptions.***

When you have researched a company and found a fit with their goals and interests, it's important to explain this match in your proposal. Be careful about the wording you use. Do not use language that implies you know exactly what the company wants. For example, phrasing such as "You will naturally be interested in this project because...." or "You must participate in this project because...." implies that you know more about the company than the managers. Show your fit with the company, but do not tell the company's managers how to think. Use wording such as "We believe you will find our program interesting because...."

- *Be accurate about your sources of funding.*

   A number of companies reported a disheartening tendency for some non-profits to inaccurately list funding sources. One non-profit agency actually included a statement in the cover letter thanking the company for previous funding, when the company never gave the non-profit so much as a nickel! Perhaps this was an honest error, in which case it shows a distressing lack of control over financial issues. At worst, it is a blatant attempt to misrepresent facts in order to perhaps gain an advantage in the decision-making process. Whatever the case, such inaccuracies are met with disdain and will severely impact your proposal.

- *Remain optimistic.*

   The work done by non-profits is critical, particularly in this era of reduced government involvement and support for addressing social problems. Although it is frustrating to deal with funders and the funding process, try to remember the good your agency is doing in the community. Corporations rely on non-profits to act as a conduit or bridge to the community. Only through non-profits can corporations successfully fund important social issues and make an impact in the community. The non-profit sector is vital to the success of corporate funding programs.

   Unfortunately, corporations cannot respond to all community needs and they must choose the few that make most sense to their business. As grantseekers, non-profits should be confident about the importance of their work. Do not take a rejection personally. Learn all you can from a denial of funding and move on to the next potential funder.

Afterword

As a non-profit agency, you are providing a wonderful service for our society! You have embraced the value of service and the need to positively impact very difficult problems. Everyday you work with issues and concerns that are just as complex as those confronting corporate executives. Your work is as valuable to our society as the work done in corporate suites and, in some cases, more valuable. I applaud your dedication and devotion to your cause, and your desire to make the world today a little better place than it was yesterday.

I hope this book has been informative and will help you find the corporate funder for your program. Even if your efforts at finding corporate funders have been unsuccessful in the past, I encourage you to use the techniques described in this book to continue your search. Somewhere out there is a corporation that is a perfect match for your program. Good luck with your search!

Linda Zukowski

APPENDICES
Table of Contents

APPENDIX I
List of Participating Corporations

AirTouch Communications Foundation

Apple Computer, Inc.

ARCO Foundation

AT&T

Bank of America

Charles Schwab & Co.

Chevron

Farmers Group, Inc.

Great Western Financial Corporation

Hewlett Packard Company

Intel Foundation

Key Bank

Levi Strauss

McDonnell Douglas Employees Community Fund, Inc.

McKesson

Mervyn's

NIKE, Inc.

Oracle

PacifiCorp Foundation

Pacific Bell Foundation

Pacific Gas and Electric Company

Portland General Electric

Ralphs Food 4 Less Foundation

SAFECO Insurance Companies

Seafirst Bank

SEGA Foundation

Silicon Graphics

Sony Pictures Entertainment

Southern California Edison & Edison International

Standard Insurance Company

Sun Microsystems Foundation, Inc.

Texaco Inc.

Transamerica Foundation

US WEST Foundation

US Bank of Washington

Wells Fargo

Weyerhaeuser Company Foundation

Appendix 2

Research Questionnaire and Responses by Region

The following questions were posed to representatives of the corporations listed in Appendix 1. Responses were based on a five point scale from **Strongly Disagree** to **Strongly Agree.** The first column under each question is a summary of responses from all companies in the survey. Responses from corporations headquartered in Oregon and Washington have been combined into the category of "Pacific Northwest" (PNW). This category also includes US WEST Foundation. Although headquartered in Colorado, this corporation has a significant charitable giving program in Washington and Oregon. The "California" (CA) category includes corporations in both the northern and southern sections of the state.

1. Cultivating a personal relationship with my company, by contacting local managers or involving our employees, is a suggested first step for non-profits seeking funding.

53% = Agreed or strongly agreed (PNW = 67%/CA = 46%)
11% = Disagreed or strongly disagreed (PNW = 0%/CA = 15%)
36% = Neither agreed nor disagreed (PNW = 33%/CA = 39%)

Responses from the Pacific Northwest tended to indicate an interest in some personal connection between corporate funder and non-profit, perhaps because of the more rural geography, the reliance on the input from local employees in these rural areas and the "small town" feel to many of the large cities. While most agreed with the statement, many California companies felt the relationship occurred over time, after the decision to fund had been made.

2. *We are more interested in funding organizations whose board members are politically connected, influential, community leaders or executives of our company.*

> **32%** = Agreed or strongly agreed (PNW = 33%/CA = 31%)
> **37%** = Disagreed or strongly disagreed (PNW = 42%/CA = 35%)
> **31%** = Neither agreed nor disagreed (PNW = 25%/CA = 34%)

The varied distribution of the responses supports the comments in the interviews which indicated that some, but not all, of the above factors are of interest to most companies.

3. *We consider our funding of non-profit organizations to be more of a strategic business investment in the community, rather than an altruistic donation to a charity.*

> **55%** = Agreed or strongly agreed (PNW = 67%/CA = 50%)
> **11%** = Disagreed or strongly disagreed (PNW = 0%/CA = 15%)
> **34%** = Neither agreed nor disagreed (PNW = 33%/CA = 35%)

The common theme was that corporate charitable giving is becoming more limited, while the number of non-profits continues to grow. Corporations cannot support every agency and so look for ways to distinguish among them. Identifying non-profits that seem to be making an impact in the community is one way of determining how to distribute corporate dollars.

4. *An excellent way for new, grassroots non-profits to initially gain my interest is to periodically send me relevant news clippings, or brief summaries of their accomplishments/awards, without requesting funding.*

> **40%** = Agreed or strongly agreed (PNW = 42%/CA = 39%)
> **45%** = Disagreed or strongly disagreed (PNW = 50%/CA = 42%)
> **15%** = Neither agreed nor disagreed (PNW = 8%/CA = 19%)

These responses were surprising given the overall concern expressed in the interviews about the lack of time to get the job done. I suggest that non-profits send the above type of information only if it is requested by the company, or if they have first asked if sending this type of information is acceptable.

5. After determining that they meet our guidelines, non-profits should call my office to discuss their project and our potential interest, before sending a proposal.

42% = Agreed or strongly agreed (PNW = 58%/CA = 35%)
47% = Disagreed or strongly disagreed (PNW = 42%/CA = 50%)
11% = Neither agreed nor disagreed (PNW = 0%/CA = 15%)

Most companies expressed a desire to be able to talk with non-profits, but many had no time to do so. As in question #1, the responses seem to indicate more of an interest in the Pacific Northwest in personal contact and building relationships as a part of the funding decision. Many companies in Oregon and Washington said they personally knew all the development officers and directors, and tended to support those agencies familiar to them. However, the demands of too little time are evident by the high "disagree" response in both regions. This question resulted in the highest "strongly disagree" response in the entire survey—39% from California, again supporting relationship building as something that occurs after funding.

6. The most effective project objectives are quantitative rather than qualitative, and include a strategy and timeline for completion.

62% = Agreed or strongly agreed (PNW = 75%/CA = 56%)
14% = Disagreed or strongly disagreed (PNW = 17%/CA = 12%)
24% = Neither agreed nor disagreed (PNW = 8%/CA = 32%)

Pacific Northwest was very much in agreement. While in California, an additional three companies would have agreed with the statement if it was worded so that both quantitative and qualitative objectives were of equal importance, and the timeline and strategy were stressed. (This would have increased the "agree" responses to 68% in California.)

7. *All requests for funding should include a description of a plan to evaluate success that is based on achievement of project objectives.*

> **81%** = Agreed or strongly agreed (PNW = 92%/CA = 76%)
> **5%** = Disagreed or strongly disagreed (PNW = 0%/CA = 8%)
> **14%** = Neither agreed nor disagreed (PNW = 8%/CA = 16%)

Responses again were similar across regions, although the Pacific Northwest was very much in agreement. Interestingly, although the importance of evaluations is evident from these responses, most companies felt this was the weakest area in the proposals they received. Some companies indicated that evaluations were most important for larger projects. Others felt that, although evaluations were important, they rarely expected to see them in proposals because non-profits had little time/money for evaluation.

8. *We are more likely to fund non-profits that have already attracted funding from a variety of other sources. We are less likely to be the first or lead funder.*

> **46%** = Agreed or strongly agreed (PNW = 75%/CA = 32%)
> **19%** = Disagreed or strongly disagreed (PNW = 0%/CA = 28%)
> **35%** = Neither agreed nor disagreed (PNW = 25%/CA = 40%)

Big differences here. Perhaps tracking with the fact that the Pacific Northwest's funding decisions involve relationships. They are less likely to fund new, unknown agencies. There also was more of a tendency for companies in Oregon and Washington to discuss their funding decisions with each other more, making it less likely, although not impossible, for a new non-profit to get corporate support without first attracting other sources of support. In California, the majority neither agreed nor disagreed with the need to first attract other funders.

9. Regardless of a non-profit's size or tenure, a detailed analysis of their budget, including cash flow and projected income, is a critical part of our funding decision.

> **73%** = Agreed or strongly agreed (PNW = 83%/CA = 68%)
> **8%** = Disagreed or strongly disagreed (PNW = 8%/CA = 8%)
> **19%** = Neither agreed nor disagreed (PNW = 9%/CA = 24%)

When looking at questions #8 and #9 together, it appears that, although financials are important in all regions, they seem to be a little less of a factor in California. This again may be due to the fact that California appears a little more willing to consider new non-profits (whose financials may not be in the best of shape).

10. When seeking our funding, the most effective non-profits convey a professional business attitude, and clearly and concisely indicate how their services match our strategic interests.

> **83%** = Agreed or strongly agreed (PNW = 83%/CA = 83%)
> **9%** = Disagreed or strongly disagreed (PNW = 17%/CA = 4%)
> **8%** = Neither agreed nor disagreed (PNW = 0%/CA = 13%)

Despite minor differences between regions, most companies agree that non-profits need to convey a professional attitude when approaching corporations.

APPENDIX 3
Resources for Researching Corporations

- ## *The Foundation Center*

  The Foundation Center provides the most comprehensive collection of information on foundation and corporate giving. The main locations are in New York, San Francisco, Washington, D.C., Cleveland and Atlanta, but smaller "cooperating collections" are located in libraries, community foundations and various other locations throughout the U.S. For the location of the collection nearest to you, call 1-800-424-9836. Most locations have staff to answer questions and guide you to the correct directories. Many also offer free orientation meetings to introduce you to the material available in the locations. There is no charge to use the material. The material cannot be removed from the location, although copying facilities are usually available for a fee. (See Appendix 5 for information on the Foundation Center's web site.)

  Not all materials are available at all locations. If you are seeking a specific document or reference, it is suggested that you call ahead to ensure its availability. Materials available at the Foundation Center libraries generally include the following:

  - *IRS Form 990-PF* on microfilm which provides fiscal data, trustees/officers, and listings of previously distributed grants for the private foundations in the state in which the library is located. (Some locations also include information on private foundations in neighboring states.)

  - annual reports, press releases, newsletters

  - foundation directories (see listing below), books and periodicals

- *FC Search: The Foundation Center's Database on CD-ROM* allows for computer research of foundations, using a number of variables including name, subject or location. (Also available for purchase from the Foundation Center. Requires IBM compatible PC, Microsoft Windows 3.1, 486DX microprocessor, 8MB memory, CD-ROM drive.)

- **Chamber of Commerce**

  The Chamber of Commerce will most likely have a list of the local corporations and the affiliates of national corporations that are headquartered in your city.

- **Corporate Funding Directories**

  The following are some of the directories which provide in-depth information on corporate foundations and corporate giving programs. Most include contact information, description of the company's funding interests, application procedures, financial data, geographic limitations and listings of recently awarded grants. (Use the directories only as guides since the information may have changed since the directory was printed. Always call the company for the most recent guidelines and application procedures.) Many of these directories are available for use in the Foundation Center or they can be purchased from the publisher:

  - *Corporate 500; The Directory of Corporate Philanthropy.* San Francisco: Datarex Corporation.

  - *Corporate Foundation Profiles.* New York: The Foundation Center. (1-800-424-9836)

  - *Corporate Giving Directory.* Michigan: The Taft Group. (1-800-877-8238)

  - *Corporate Giving Yellow Pages.* Michigan: The Taft Group. (List of contact information only.) (1-800-877-8238)

  - *Directory of International Corporate Giving in America and Abroad.* Michigan: The Taft Group. (1-800-877-8238)

- *1998 IEG Sponsorship Source Book.* Illinois: International Events Group. (312-944-1727) (A directory of corporate sponsorship.)

- *National Directory of Corporate Giving.* New York: The Foundation Center. (1-800-424-9836)

- *The Directory of Corporate and Foundation Givers.* Michigan: The Taft Group. (1-800-877-8238)

- *National Directory of Corporate Public Affairs.* Washington, D.C. Columbia Books. (202-898-0662)

- *Giving by Industry: A Reference Guide to the New Corporate Philanthropy.* Virginia: Capitol Publications. (1-800-655-5597)

- **Periodicals**

Available by subscription, the following periodicals provide current information on trends in corporate philanthropy. Funding interests of specific corporations are described in each issue. Subscriptions are expensive, so I suggest that you call and request a sample copy to ensure the material meets your needs.

- *Corporate Philanthropy Report.* Virginia: Capitol Publications Inc. (1-800-655-5597)

- *Chronicle of Philanthropy.* Washington, D.C.: The Chronicle of Higher Education. (Also available online. See Appendix 5.) (202-466-1234)

- *Corporate Giving Watch.* Michigan: The Taft Group. (1-800-877-8238)

The *New York Times* and *Wall Street Journal* are excellent sources of current business news and trends. Also, the business section of your local newspaper is a good source of information about current issues affecting corporations in your area and can provide clues about their funding interests. (See Appendix 5 for newspapers on the Internet.) *Forbes, Fortune* and *Business Week* magazines are also good sources of information on emerging business trends and are usually available in local libraries.

I suggest you read or skim the business section of a newspaper each day. This will keep you aware of significant corporate activities in your area and general business trends. Learn to read business news with the purpose of assessing the impact, if any, to your non-profit and your area of concern.

• *Dun and Bradstreet*

Available in most libraries, a source for general background information on businesses. It will not give information on corporate foundations or giving programs, but it will provide extensive background on the company including: names of the company's executives, main address, type of business and financial data. This is a good place to begin researching companies in your community. (Also available online, see Appendix 5.)

• *Databases and Online Services*

Databases and online services are expensive. New non-profits or those with a limited budget can find the same information in the above mentioned corporate directories. But if you have the budget, the online services make researching of companies easier and quicker. Since most of the services include annual updates (some for an additional fee), the information is more accurate than old copies of directories. However, even online services may contain outdated information, so be sure to call the company for current information.

– *Corporate Foundations and Giving.* Virginia: Capitol Publications. (800-655-5597)
Database of 4,000 corporate philanthropic programs, updated annually. Available for Macintosh, DOS and Windows.

– *Grants on Disk.* Michigan: The Taft Group. (1-800-877-8238)
CD-ROM listing of over 150,000 grants awarded by more than 5,000 foundations and corporate giving programs, updated quarterly. Available for Windows.

- *Prospector's Choice.* Michigan: The Taft Group. (1-800-877-8238)
  CD-ROM listing of over 10,000 foundations and corporate
  giving programs. Includes biographical information on the company's officers and a sample of grants made by each company.
  Updated annually. Also available on diskette.

- *Sources of Foundations.* Virginia: Capitol Publications.
  (1-800-655-5597)
  Profiles more than 13,000 corporate and private foundations and
  includes names of foundation trustees and directors. Updated
  annually. Available in CD-ROM, DOS, Macintosh and Windows.

- *GrantScape: Corporate Foundations and Giving.* Virginia: Capitol
  Publications. (1-800-655-5597)
  Database of more than 2,300 corporate foundations and direct
  giving programs. Updated annually. Available in CD-ROM,
  Macintosh and Windows.

APPENDIX 4

Researching Matching Gift Programs

The following are resources containing information on corporate matching gift programs. When beginning a matching gift program, do not forget to check with your donors and clients. They may be able to inform you about the matching gift programs offered by their employers. Matching gift programs change frequently, so check with donors and clients every year.

- **Books and Directories**

  - *Guidelines for the Administration of Matching Gift Programs.* Washington, D.C.: Council for the Advancement and Support of Education. (1-800-554-8536)
  This book defines methods for implementing a matching gift program.

  - *Matching Gift Details Directory.* Washington, D.C.: Council for the Advancement and Support of Education. (Also available as software. See below.) (1-800-554-8536)
  This directory describes the matching gift programs offered by 1,000 parent and 5,300 subsidiary companies.

- **Computer Databases and Online Services**

  - *Matchfinder.* Charleston, S.C.: Blackbaud. (1-800-443-9441) Provides online information about corporate matching gift programs, and also helps a non-profit use its prospect lists to identify potential donors who work for companies with matching gift programs. Updated annually. Windows 95, Windows NT or Novell Netware.

- *Matching Gift Details for Windows.* Washington, D.C.: Council for the Advancement and Support of Education. (1-800-554-8536)
  Describes the matching gift program of 6,000 corporations. Windows 95, Windows NT and Windows 3.1.

- *GiftPlus Online.* Virginia: Higher Education Publications. (1-800-681-4438)
  Continually updated information on the matching gift programs of about 9,000 companies.

- **Newsletter**

  - *Matching Gifts Notes.* Washington, D.C.: Council for the Advancement and Support of Education. Published quarterly.

Appendix 5
Internet Resources

The Internet is an excellent source of background information on corporations, corporate charitable giving and fund raising in general. As with any Internet search, however, you can easily become "lost in cyberspace" and overwhelmed with data. After sifting through much data, I have found the following web sites to be the most informative. Although much of the Internet data on corporate foundations is also available in printed form, Internet information can be updated more frequently than printed corporate funding directories. In addition, online newspapers allow for quick scanning of national and local news sources to identify current issues affecting specific industries or specific companies.

- *Council on Foundations* (http://www.cof.org)
  Provides links to 150 foundation sites. Frequently asked questions (FAQ's) discuss corporate community involvement and corporate giving.

- *The Grantsmanship Center*
  (http://www.tgci.com/foundations/corpfdn.htm)
  Provides links to corporate foundation web sites. The home page offers links to government grants, non-profit training and various grantmakers.

- *Independent Sector* (http://www.indepsec.org)
  Independent Sector is a national coalition of voluntary organizations, foundations and corporate giving programs with an interest in philanthropy. This web site provides general information and statistics on all aspects of America's philanthropic and volunteer sector.

- *Southern California Association for Philanthropy*
  (http://www.scap.org)
  Links to corporate and private foundations in California.

- *PRSPCT-L* (http://www.bucknell.edu/boeke/work/info.html)
  A free electronic discussion group that provides a way for users to
  share information and problems on all aspects of grantwriting
  and research of funders. Subscribers receive the monthly online
  newsletter called *Internet Prospector.*

- *The Foundation Center* (http://fdncenter.org/)
  Provides links to web sites of over 50 corporate funders, as well as
  private foundations. The "reference desk" page provides answers
  to frequently asked questions (FAQ's) about corporate giving.
  The home page provides information on the foundation center
  library closest to you.

- *Foundations Online* (http://www.foundations.org/page2.html)
  Offered by the Northern California Community Foundation,
  this site has links to 60 corporate and private foundations, with
  many, but not all, located in California.

- *Philanthropy Journal Online* (http://www.philanthropy-journal.org/)
  Provides links to corporate and private foundations.

- *Hoover's Company Capsules* (http://hooveweb.hoovers.com/)
  Free information on 5,000 of the world's largest corporations
  including contact information, sales, employment, stock quotes
  and links to more information.

- *CorpTech* (http://www.corptech.com/)
  Database of 45,000 high-tech companies of various sizes.

- *Corporate Information*
  (http://www.corporateinformation.com/uspriv.html)
  Links to various databases containing corporate information
  including:

  - *Forbes 500 Top Private Companies:* background data on
    corporations.

- *Thomas Register:* index of manufactures in the U.S. and Canada. Searches can be done by company name or product.

- *Infoseek Company Information:* news stories, descriptions and home pages of 45,000 companies.

- *Companies Online:* basic company descriptions, including sales, number of employees, parent company, contact names and e-mail addresses.

- *Big Book:* names, addresses, phone numbers of millions of American businesses.

Online Newspapers, Periodicals and News Services

• *The Chronicle of Philanthropy* (http://philanthropy.com)
Comprehensive summary of fund raising news, nationwide fund raising conferences and workshops and grant deadlines.

• *American City Business Journals* (http://www.amcity.com)
Provides access to business newspapers in 35 cities, including Portland, Oregon, Seattle and San Francisco.

• *Dun & Bradstreet*
(http://www.dnb.com/dbis/dnbhome.htm)
Offers business reports online for a fee.

• *My Virtual Reference Desk* (http://www.refdesk.com/paper.html)
Links to hundreds of worldwide online newspapers, Associated Press and Reuters. There is so much information here, it can easily become overwhelming.

• *CNN Interactive* (http://www.cnn.com/SEARCH/index.html)
Offers key word searches to review current corporate news stories.

• *Wall Street Journal Interactive* (http://www.wsj.com)
Fee for an online subscription.

• *Seattle Times* (http://www.seattletimes.com/topstories)
Archived stories since 1996.

- *San Francisco Examiner & Chronicle*
  (http://www.sfgate.com/search/)
  Archived stories since January 1995.

- *New York Times* (http://www.nytimes.com)
  Free registration available to anyone in the U.S.

- *Los Angeles Times*
  (http://www.latimes.com/HOME/RESEARCH/ARCHIVES/)
  Free search and brief summary of headlines from 1990. Fee to
  download or print the entire story.

- *Web Bazaar* (http://www.1-web-bazaar-plaza.com/newspapers/)
  Links to newspapers from over 20 cities across the U.S., including
  Albuquerque, Denver, Juneau, Las Vegas, Los Angeles, Maui,
  Phoenix, Portland, Oregon, Salt Lake City, San Diego, San
  Francisco and Seattle.

APPENDIX 6
Recommended Reading

The following resources were not used in the writing of this book, however, they provide information on corporate funding of non-profit organizations and may be helpful to anyone seeking additional perspectives:

Andreasen, Alan R. "Profits for Nonprofits: Find a Corporate Partner." *Harvard Business Review.* November-December 1996, pp. 47-59.

Blum, Debra E., and Gray, Susan. "Hot Firms Cool Toward Philanthropy." *The Chronicle of Philanthropy.* May 15, 1997, pp. 9-14.

Dickey, Marilyn. "Free Money: How Charities Can Make the Most of Matching Gifts." *The Chronicle of Philanthropy.* March 6, 1997, pp. 40-42.

Knauft, E.B. *Profiles of Effective Corporate Giving Programs.* Washington, D.C.: Independent Sector, 1985.

Newman, M.W. "Getting Through the Door." *Advancing Philanthropy.* Winter 1996-97, pp. 19-23.

Sheridan Associates and Zimmerman Associates. *Study of Cause-Related Marketing.* Washington, D.C.: Independent Sector, 1988.

Smith, Craig. *Giving by Industry: A Reference Guide to the New Corporate Philanthropy.* Alexandria, Virginia: Capitol Publications, 1996.

Smith, Craig. "The New Corporate Philanthropy." *Harvard Business Review.* May-June 1994, p. 116.

Stead, Deborah. "Corporations, Classrooms and Commercialism." *The New York Times,* January 5, 1997, Education Life Supplement, pp. 30-45.

APPENDIX 7
Free Proposal Critique

Would you like a little professional help with your proposal? Buyers of this book can take advantage of a free proposal critique offered by the author of this book and professional grantwriter, Linda Zukowski.

If you are interested in a free critique, rewrite your proposal or letter of inquiry according to the suggestions given in this book. Then send the document to the address listed below. Please include a stamped, self-addressed envelope large enough for your proposal. Since the free critique is available only to buyers of this book, you must also tear out this page and include it with your request. Photocopies of this page will not be accepted. Also include proof of purchase of this book—a receipt or a copy of the canceled check. Requests received without this page and proof of purchase of this book will be returned without comment.

Mail your proposal, a stamped, self-addressed envelope, proof of purchase and this page to:

EarthWrites
Linda Zukowski
409 N. Pacific Coast Hwy. #423
Redondo Beach, California 90277

All proposals must be word processed or typewritten (15 pages maximum). Handwritten copies will not be accepted. You will receive your proposal back with comments written in the margins, so send a copy and not the original. It is suggested that you send a copy of the exact proposal you plan to submit, so that comments can be made about its format, as well as its content. You can include a list of attachments, but do not send the attachments themselves.

This offer is valid for a critique of one proposal only. Additional proposal critiques are available for $95 each. Mail the additional proposals, stamped, self-addressed envelope and a check to "EarthWrites Consulting" to the above address.

Please send proposals by U.S. Mail, and not by fax or e-mail.

(Due to the large volume of requests, we are unable to provide return postage. Any proposals received without a stamped, self-addressed envelope will be discarded.)

EarthWrites

I hope you have found this book to be interesting and useful. If you have any questions or comments about the material in this book, or if would like to purchase additional copies of this book, please contact me at the address below.

Also, please send me your name and address if you would like to be included on our mailing list and informed when my corporate grantwriting workshops are scheduled in a location near you.

EarthWrites
Linda Zukowski
409 N. Pacific Coast Hwy. #423
Redondo Beach, California 90277
e-mail: LZukowski@aol.com
web site: http://www.earthwrites.com

Index

Order Form

Please send the following book by Linda M. Zukowski:

Item	Quantity	Unit Cost	Total Cost
Fistfuls of Dollars: ***Fact and Fantasy About*** ***Corporate Charitable Giving***		$14.95	$
	Sales Tax Please add 8.25% for books shipped to California addresses.		$
	Shipping $4.00 for the first book and $2.00 for each additional book.		$
		Total Enclosed	$

Please make the check or money order out to EarthWrites, and mail it with this completed form to:

EarthWrites
Linda Zukowski
409 N. Pacific Coast Hwy. #423
Redondo Beach, California 90277

Ship the book(s) to:

Company name

Name

Address

City   *State*   *Zip*

Telephone

Sorry, no credit card or C.O.D. orders.
If you are not satisfied with the book, it may be returned for a full refund.

Order Form

Please send the following book by Linda M. Zukowski:

Item	Quantity	Unit Cost	Total Cost
Fistfuls of Dollars: ***Fact and Fantasy About*** ***Corporate Charitable Giving***		$14.95	$
	Sales Tax Please add 8.25% for books shipped to California addresses.		$
	Shipping $4.00 for the first book and $2.00 for each additional book.		$
		Total Enclosed	$

Please make the check or money order out to EarthWrites, and mail it with this completed form to:

EarthWrites
Linda Zukowski
409 N. Pacific Coast Hwy. #423
Redondo Beach, California 90277

Ship the book(s) to:

_____
Company name

_____
Name

_____
Address

_____
City   *State*   *Zip*

_____
Telephone

Sorry, no credit card or C.O.D. orders.
If you are not satisfied with the book, it may be returned for a full refund.